The VICTORIOUS STATE of MIND

To Myea,
May God Bless
you as you
walk out this!
Next season of
Peace & Joy

LAKEISHA DIXON

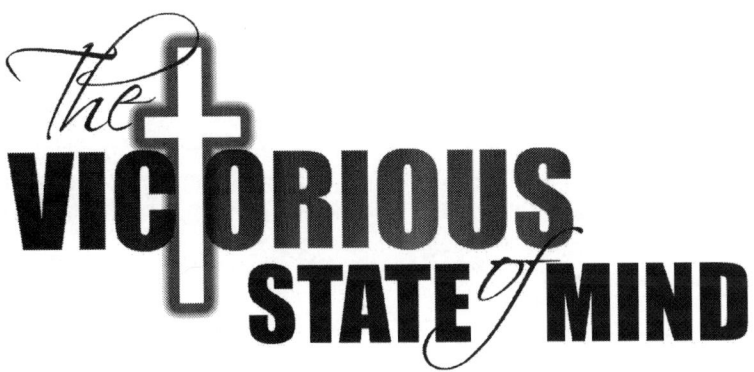

The VICTORIOUS STATE of MIND

Positioning
Yourself to
Receive
the Promises
of God

LAKEISHA DIXON

Victorious
Christian Book Publishing
www.lakeishadixon.com

Table *of* Contents

vic·to·ri·ous

1. Having won a victory; triumphant: having defeated an adversary.
2. Of or characterized by victory;
3. Being the winner in a contest or struggle;
4. Characteristic of or expressing a sense of victory or fulfillment

Dedication

This book, *"The Victorious State Of Mind"*, is dedicated to the late Sarah Smith (Granny) and Estell Dixon (Grandma). These two lovely women of God were my grandmothers and they built the foundation for Christ in my life. They understood the power of prayer and perseverance. I was raised in Church and experienced God's love and faithfulness at an early age. I know that the mantle of prayer and inspiration for the things of God was embedded in my heart because of what was shown and taught to me by these two women.

Sarah Smith was a grandmother, who loved her grandchildren and was determined to see us walk in the love and adoration of Christ. We did not have a choice on whether or not we were going to Church. It was a requirement to attend Sunday school and stay after church on 1st Sundays to eat and fellowship with the congregation. My Granny always baked the cakes and pies for the church. Now, I am the one who is praying, cooking, and baking cakes and pies for family and friends to enjoy!

Until We Met Again In Heaven!

Lakeisha Dixon

Introduction

The Process

*"... my message and preaching (are) very plain. Rather than using
clever and persuasive speeches, I (rely) only on the power of the
Holy Spirit"*
1 Corinthians 2:4 (NLT)

It has been a burning passion of mine to write a book that would bring
God's people to a place of victory in their lives. Some of us have been
abused, mistreated and have even allowed others to speak negatively
into and over our lives. We have received and believed what others
have said about us. Now it's time for you to believe and receive what
God has said about you. God has great things in store for you. It is time
for you to get in position to surrender so that you can receive all that
God has prepared for your life. As long as the earth remains, and you
remain a part of it, you will be stretched, pulled and pushed. It's all a
part of faith and character building. How you react in these moments
of growth will determine your victory. Your faith, praise and worship
will determine your outcome.

This project has been a labor of love and is designed to be a "how-to"
guide to teach you how to apply the word of God that is already in your
heart, to your life. It is an easy read, but it is not for the faint of heart!
It is my prayer that as you read my testimony and the steps that I took
to become an overcomer – a truly VICTORIOUS PERSON in God –
that you, too, will see what steps you can take in your own life to walk
in the victory that has already been won for you!

*"Sin will be rampant everywhere, and the love of many will grow
cold. But the one who endures to the end will be saved."*
Matthew 24:12-13 (NLT)

As you read through each chapter of this book you will be forced to ask yourself questions. Some of the questions will be tough for you to confront, but hang in there. There will be a spiritual awakening to righteousness and to the unveiling of the truth of God's Word. Your life is about to change! Your mind will be renewed. Your heart will become open to the things of God. You will see yourself as God sees you. You will have a fresh excitement about life. Chains and shackles will be destroyed and broken off of your life. You will become liberated. You will soar like an eagle and never go back to your old way of thinking and living again! You were born to win and not to give up on life. No matter what you may be going through right now, continue to fight the good fight of faith.

"For this battle is not yours but God's."
2 Chronicles 20:15

Many Christians are losing the battle because we are fighting it while wounded, naked, exposed and unequipped. You must always be prepared for battle by putting on the whole armor of God. I am here to tell you that there is no need for you to keep fighting battles in your own strength. Get ready to walk into the best days of your life! God is going to blow your mind. You haven't seen nor heard anything yet! I declare that you still have more blessings with your name on them! It's time to unclog your spiritual pipeline so that the blessings of God can flow to you unhindered and uncontaminated. I speak it over your life right now! I declare and decree that after you have read this book, your life will be forever changed because of the supernatural experience that you will have encountered with the Almighty God, in Jesus' name!

In the name of Jesus, I declare that
The time is now for you to stop living in a defeated state of mind!
The time is now for you to say, "I am winning because Christ has already won!"
The time is now for you to say, "I shall live and not die, to proclaim the glory of the Lord!"
The time is now for you to take up your cross and follow Christ!

The time is now for you to lose that victim mentality and declare that you are a VICTOR!!
The time is now for you to beat the devil out of your life through prayer and the authority you already have in Christ Jesus!
The time is now for you to heal old wounds and to live the best life that God intended for you to live.

It's time for you to be restored, delivered, and healed. It's time to create your own atmosphere with the power of your words!

*"Eye has not seen, nor ear heard, nor have entered into the heart of man, the things which God has prepared for those who love Him" - **1 Corinthians 2:9***

No more masking and suppressing your pain. No more hiding and crying in shame. It is time to allow God to destroy the yokes of bondage from your life so that you can break loose and break forth. Follow me as I follow Christ, as we begin our journey together towards Victorious Living!

Lakeisha Dixon

Chapter 1

Purpose
"The Calling"

Have you ever thought about giving up? I know I have. The truth of the matter is we all have thought about giving up in our lives at some point or another. Some of us have thought about giving up on our jobs, giving up in ministry, giving up in our marriages, giving up on people and even giving up on our dreams, simply because we have allowed the enemy, and other people's opinions, to distract us from God's original plan and purpose for our lives. We were created to complete our assignments and fulfill our purpose.

> *To everything there is a season,*
> *a time for every purpose under heaven.*
> ***Ecclesiastes 3:1***

For most of us, the world as we know it has changed dramatically since we were kids. No more sitting in the house waiting for the phone to ring because now we have cell phones and text messages. No more running home and waiting for your favorite shows to start because DVRs have put "primetime" on your time, making TV schedules more convenient for each individual viewer. However, life is not always about having your way right away. Life is about learning, growing,

discovering and changing. Everything in life was created for and with a purpose. For instance, a butter knife was created to spread butter; not for you to use as a screw driver. Whenever something is created for a specific reason, it will never be able to function properly outside of its original purpose, which is defined as:

1. The reason for which something exists or is done, made, or used.
2. an intended or desired result; end; aim; goal.

As we look at the definition of purpose, we can clearly see that we were created for something. You were created to be a living organism. God had a plan for you in mind even before you were born. We were all created, made, designed for something. In other words, we are not problems; we are solutions waiting to happen. You are useful; not useless. You are valuable to the kingdom of God and God knew exactly what He was doing when He made you. You are not a mistake. You are supposed to be here. You were crafted, by the hands of God and placed on this earth for a purpose. Whether you know it or believe it, or not, you have a purpose. Once you recognize and accept this basic truth, then there won't be anything in this world that will be able to stop you from pursuing it nor from becoming what God created you to be. Yes, there will be road blocks, stumbling blocks, failures and moments of weakness, but you were designed to conquer them all. You will not be defeated. Yes, you have a reason to live, a reason to breathe and a reason to exist. Someone is depending on your gifts, talents and abilities to push them forward and to see them through. Someone is waiting for you to help them discover who they are in Christ. This is not a season for you to be confused or discouraged; this is the time for you to be still and trust that God has a purpose for your life, to be carried out through various assignments.

(David) sent out spies to verify the report of Saul's arrival.
1Samuel 26:4 (NLT)

Moses gave the men these instructions as he sent them out to explore the land: "Go north through the Negev into the hill country.
Numbers 13:17 (NLT)

Your assignment is that task or mission that you have been assigned to. It is bigger than your capacity to know how you will bring it to pass. You have to trust God and believe that if He called you to do it, then He will provide the resources, tools, finances and any other provisions you need to bring it to fruition. Do you know what your assignment is? Have you completed your assignment? If, your answer is "NO", then why would you ever think about giving up? We all have been given a divine assignment and your assignment is closely related to the vision that God has already placed in you.

Write the vision and make it plain on tablets, that he may run who reads it. For the vision is yet for an appointed time. But at the end it will speak and it will not lie. Though it tarries, wait for it; it will surely come, it will not tarry.
Habakkuk 2:2-3

Vision is defined as:

1. The act or power of sensing with the eye;
2. The act or power of anticipating that which will or may come to be: prophetic vision.
3. Something seen or otherwise perceived during such an experience; Imaginative conception.

Vision is the long view of your purpose and assignments. It allows you to see beyond what your natural eyes and carnal mind can perceive and allows you to see what can be, what will be, and what is to come. We often lose sight of our vision because we do not see the end result every day. In the book of Habakkuk, we are instructed to write the vision in a plain way. This may seem oversimplified, or even unnecessary, however, science has proven that writing things down forces the brain to organize important elements of information into categories, such as assignments, which are necessary to complete in order for you to fulfill your purpose.

The scripture goes on to remind us that the vision will be made manifest. At times it may seem that all of your efforts are in vain and your vision may appear to be delayed or late but hold on! God has not

forgotten you. He is not slack concerning His promises. If He said it then it must, it shall, and it will come to pass. God is a faithful God. He is the only truth you will ever need. You must find a way to see your vision every day. Try reading it out loud, or creating a vision board, and begin to visualize yourself living it, doing it and being it. Try cutting out pictures of things related to your vision and place them strategically throughout your home and other personal spaces, so that you can continually remind yourself of what God has promised you. Do not lose sight of what God has called you to do. The devil is trying to undermine the plan and purpose of God for your life. He knows that if he can distract you and cause you to doubt what God says that he can get you to abort the birthing process. Notice that I said *he* can get *you* to abort the birthing process. The devil has no authority in your life and can only go as far as you allow him to. I am here to tell you, though, DO NOT waiver, DO NOT quit and DO NOT cave in. When applied, instructions that are followed will open the door to a life without limitation and borders.

But Samuel replied, "What is more pleasing to the LORD:
your burnt offerings and sacrifices or your obedience to his voice?
Listen! Obedience is better than sacrifice,
and submission is better than offering the fat of ram.
1 Samuel 15:22 (NLT)

If He said it, you can take it to the bank and cash it and you won't have to worry about insufficient funds or stop payments!

So is my word that goes out from my mouth: It will not return to me
empty, but will accomplish what I desire and achieve the purpose for
which I sent it.
Isaiah 55:11

By now, you are probably saying, "But Lakeisha: "You just don't know what I've been going through lately."

"You don't know how my finances have dried
up and died."
"You don't know how I lost my job and can't

4

find another one."
"You don't know how tired I am of living in a state of complacency."
"You don't know how my kids are acting up and running wild."
"You don't know how my marriage is sinking and falling apart."
"You don't know how I have been crying myself to sleep because I am so lonely and desire to be married."
"You don't know how I am sick in my body and the medicine won't help."

My answer to that is: "I don't need to know because God knows!" No matter what problem you may have, God has a solution for it. He is the Master Problem Solver. There's no problem that Jesus can't handle because He is possible in impossible situations. God will not put more on you than you can bear.

No temptation has seized you except what is common to man. And God is faithful; he will not let you be tempted beyond what you can bear. But when you are tempted, he will also provide a way out so that you can stand up under it.
1 Corinthian 10:13 (NIV)

Hallelujah! Let me encourage you! I love this verse because it reminds us that "God is FAITHFUL." God is saying there is nothing that you can ever go through that He is not fully aware of. He will not allow you to be tempted beyond what you can bear. Guess what, Baby? You are stronger than you think; you are wiser than you thought; and these trials and tribulations are strengthening you so hold on and don't let go! Again, I ask you, have you ever thought about giving up?

I am going to get a little personal here. I share my testimony with you because I understand my purpose. It is not by accident or coincidence that YOU are reading these words; it is by providence. God loves you and He sent me to remind and encourage you. He has not forgotten you! There was more than one time in my life, when I wanted to give

up. In 1997, I was 18 years old and had just finished high school when I was diagnosed with Severe Plaque Psoriasis; a non-contagious inflammatory skin disease characterized by recurring dark brown patches covered with silvery scales. In the same way that your teeth can become discolored, and the health of your gums can be negatively affected by a filmy buildup, dead skin cells can build up on your skin, causing discomfort, discoloration and pain. When you first hear this, it might sound like something that is not so serious. I mean, it's just skin, right? You can put on make-up to cover it up and you can still be cute, right? What is Lakeisha whining about? It is not that serious! Well consider this: skin is the largest and, arguably, one of the most important organs in the body. In addition to protecting you from things like radiation from the sun and fluorescent lights, irritants, such as perfumes and soaps, and other toxins that we come into contact with on a daily basis, the skin is a vital component of both our immune and elimination systems. Just think about that for a moment. When you perspire, that is your skin helping to remove certain toxins from your body, as well as regulating your body temperature so that you don't overheat. When you shiver, that is the body's way of replacing heat lost through your skin to keep you from freezing. What would you look like, how would you feel, what might happen to you if you lost all of your skin right now?

Remember, I was only 18 years old and fresh out of high school, ready to start living my life. I was sure that whatever this annoyance was that was happening to my skin could be easily fixed with a cream or a shot and then I'd be on my way. However, that isn't what happened for me. Hearing the diagnosis was distressing enough, but can you imagine my horror and confusion when my dermatologist told me that there was "No Cure" for my condition? I was devastated! Up to that point, I had been healthy and vibrant, active in my church and community, doing well in school and looking forward to college and all of the new experiences that the world had to offer me! I grew up in Miami, Florida, where the temperature and the humidity were always just about the same. HOT! Needless to say, most of the clothes that I wore were short sleeved, or short pants, or skirts. Imagine now having to cover up from neck to ankles in 90° temperatures with 100% humidity! Not to mention what a skin condition like that could do to a young woman's self-esteem. I had blossomed into a beautiful young woman, was looking forward to dating and beginning my life as a young adult and college student and then BOOM – out of nowhere, with those two little words, this dermatologist completely altered, revamped, and redirected my life. I felt betrayed by God and by my grannies. I had been a good girl. I had done everything that they told me to do. I kept myself pure and my virtue was intact. Why would God let this happen to ME???

My journey with psoriasis began immediately after the diagnosis. On the day that I was diagnosed, about 25% of my body was covered in scaly, flaky skin. It wasn't long before it seemed like my life was taking another turn for the worst. Within 2 months, my body was completely covered in scaly skin and sores. Let that sink in for a moment. 18-year old college freshman completely covered in scaly skin and sores. That's when reality began to sink in for me, and what I thought would be a manageable condition, turned into dozens of trips to the doctor's office, bleeding scaly skin, skin biopsies, steroid injections and creams, UVB lighting treatments, the same medication used in the treatment of chemotherapy patients, allergic reactions, liver biopsy, trips to a psychiatrist, and a visit to a plastic surgeon for advice. Despite all of my best efforts, though, my skin still looked horrible and I was in constant, mind-numbing pain. My doctors were running out of ideas and had already run out of answers. At this point, they were really "practicing" medicine – ON ME!

Simple, everyday tasks, such as showering, became painful reminders of what my life had become. Water was like acid on my skin. I was miserable, my entire abdomen was completely raw; my scalp was covered in scales and all my hair fell out. At times, I could hardly walk because the pain was so bad. I always felt weak and like I was on the verge of passing out. I fell into a deep depression that lasted for about 6 months. During that time, the devil's voice became very loud. He tried to convince me that death had to be better than all of the pain I was in, and I started to believe him at one point. I wanted to give up and just die. My skin wasn't able to protect me in the way that it was designed to, and I found myself slipping into episodes of convulsions and shock. My body started going into shock. For a moment, the devil

had me believing that I had no reason to live. I even remember praying and asking God to take my life. I was so low and oppressed; I couldn't see a way out. There were many sleepless nights, tossing and turning, and crying out to God for rest, for peace and for comfort. I was in a valley of hopelessness. My faith was shaken. I was even beginning to believe the voice of the enemy at that time, I started listening to a lying demon that was telling me I was ugly, and that no one would want to date me; that I had no reason to keep living, and the biggest lie of all, that I would never be healed. He began to accuse God, saying things like, "Look at what God has done to you." It was at that point that God whispered "I am with you." I remembered my truth, which is that I am a blood-bought believer who is already healed! I am here to remind you that anytime the devil is talking to you and you are able to hear him, then that means he has risen too far up out of his place; he belongs under your feet, not in your face!

We are hard pressed on every side, yet not crushed; we are perplexed, but not in despair; persecuted, but not forsaken; struck down, but not destroyed.
2 Corinthians 4:8-9

Now, I thank God for everything that I went through. Not only did it build my character, but it increased my faith. Had my faith not been shaken I would have never truly known the meaning of "unshakable faith." I was not crushed, destroyed nor forsaken. God was with me every step of the way. I came to realize that ultimately it was not about how long I was in the valley, but what I was doing while I was there. I had to remember that trouble don't last always! For every valley, there is a mountaintop! It is when you are in a valley that you can best look up and see the hand of God moving on your behalf. Trials and tests are only a sign that God still has His hands on you. Keep in mind, the greater the stretch, the greater the assignment; the greater the assignment, the greater the testimony, which will touch lives and plant seeds into the minds and hearts of God's people. Allow me to encourage you, my friend, with these words: "It's after the storm that you can see the rainbow. Whenever there's a test, there will always be a testimony". Hallelujah!

My brethren, count it all joy when you fall into various trials, know that the testing of your faith produces patience. But let patience have its perfect work, that you may be perfect and complete, lacking nothing.
James 1:2-4

"We will never outgrow warfare. We must simply learn to fight."
Dr. Mike Murdock

I know that it sounds like victory already, but that isn't the end of my story – God wasn't done with me just yet! One day while riding home from a doctor's visit, God began to minister to my heart through one of Donnie McClurkin's songs, "Stand". As I sang the words of the song along with him, God began to rain in my spirit. As I belted out "what do you do, when you've done all you can and it seems like you can't make it through? Child you just stand! Through the storm, through the rain, through the hurt and through the pain. You just stand." I could feel the love of God moving over my body and through my soul. I began to praise God with a voice of triumph! I shouted, I cried, I repented and I worshiped. I could hear the voice of the Holy Spirit saying "God won't put more on you than you can bear Lakeisha. It won't be long before your troubles are over Lakeisha. I created you to be the head and not the tail. You just hold on. I have not forgotten you." It was at that moment that I said to myself, "devil you are a liar and the fathers of lies. You cannot and will not have control over my life. I may be broken now but I serve a God that is a heart mender and a mind regulator. I know a man by the name of Jesus who died on the cross on Calvary and made me free. He healed me from the bondage of sin, sickness and disease."

My grannies instilled in me the strength to FIGHT with all of my might by simply standing on the Word of God – the only Truth that I needed. I almost let the facts and circumstances surrounding my situation cloud out my truth, which is that my battle had already been won! My freedom, my peace, my comfort and my healing were all made complete on Calvary!

But he [was] wounded for our transgressions, [he was] bruised for our iniquities: the chastisement of our peace [was] upon him; and with his stripes we are healed.
Isaiah 53:5 (KJV)

My faith was stirred up! I began to look at myself in the mirror and declare that I was healed by the Blood of Jesus! I opened my mouth and bound the spirit of sickness, disease, affliction and infirmity from my life, and spoke liberation, restoration, healing, and soundness of mind. I declared wholeness and miracles over my life. I began going back to church and allowing the WORD of God to penetrate the very core of my heart. I began to speak life into and over my own life. I received blessings and refused curses. I studied and buried myself in what the Word of God said about me and about my situation. I then took control of my own medical care. I started telling the doctors how I really felt about the treatments I wanted to use and try. I even told them that they were to be mindful of the words they used, and the attitudes that they carried into the room with them when speaking over my life. I began to speak to the pain that was racking my body and telling myself that it wouldn't be like that always. I began to see myself as God saw me, and declared that I have the victory over sickness and disease. I remembered one of His many promises:

"For I know the plans I have for you," declares the LORD,
"plans to prosper you and not to harm you,
plans to give you hope and a future."
Jeremiah 29:11

In other words, God knew my expected end – and so did the devil, who wanted to devour me and sift me like wheat. He knew even then that I was a major threat to him because he knew that I would be sharing my testimony with you - and was trying to take me out. Thank God for His mercy! I am so happy that God won't ever give the devil permission to take your life.

And the LORD said to Satan, "Behold, all that he has is in your power; only do not lay a hand on his person. "So Satan went out from the presence of the LORD.
Job 1:12

The enemy can only touch your *things;* God will never give him permission to have your life. *You* may give him your life, but God won't. I am so happy that God saw me better than I saw myself. He knew that there was greatness inside of me because he put it there. He sees Himself on the inside of me. Thank you Jesus! The enemy was trying to come against my mind because he knew that if he could get me to question God that I would be incapable of trusting the Word of God, and my faith would have never worked.

You are of God, little children, and have overcome them, because He who is in you is greater than he who is in the world.
1 John 4:4

God was greater in me than my adversary. You see, the devil wanted me to give up because he knew that one day I would be sitting in my bed, writing this book, sharing my testimony and people like you would be set free from the bondage of their situation and circumstances. The enemy knew that the Word of God was bound in my heart and that one day I would become a powerful force against his kingdom. He did not want you reading these words, which are like seeds inside your heart, mind and spirit that would eventually take root and birth out visions and dreams. The enemy did not want you to say, "If Lakeisha can do it then so can I! I can win and overcome, too."

Hallelujah!!!!
I am here to tell you
That you shall not give up!
You shall have peace!
You shall have joy!
You will not be defeated and you are not a failure!
God loves you and there's no devil in hell that can ever stop God from blessing you.

You have a purpose in life – even if you don't know what it is yet. Each purpose requires certain assignments to be carried out in order to achieve your ultimate goal. You have an assignment to do something, be something and to have something. Never underestimate the value and worth that God places on you. There is nobody like you. When

God created you, He had only you on His mind. He literally breathed Himself into you. Don't allow the enemy to get you to abort God's original plan and purpose for your life. Remember, the only power that the devil has in your life is the power of suggestion. He cannot *make* you do anything.

Do you remember the biblical account of Esau and Jacob, twin boys born to the patriarch Isaac? One of the things that stood out to me in this particular story was Esau, the oldest brother, selling his birthright to Jacob for a bowl of soup. That might not mean a lot to us in modern times; however, during biblical times the birthright meant everything. The birthright was bestowed upon the eldest son and with it came the blessing of the father and a double portion of an inheritance. This was the system for passing on wealth to the generations. It also established the eldest son as the patriarch of the family after the father passed away, which meant that the younger siblings would be subject to, or have to serve, the eldest.

Now Jacob cooked a stew; and Esau came in from the field, and he was weary. And Esau said to Jacob, "Please feed me with that same red stew, for I am weary." Therefore his name was called Edom. But Jacob said, "Sell me your birthright as of this day." And Esau said, "Look, I am about to die; so what is this birthright to me?" Then Jacob said, "Swear to me as of this day." So he swore to him, and sold his birthright to Jacob. And Jacob gave Esau bread and stew of lentils; then he ate and drank, arose, and went his way. Thus Esau despised his birthright.
Genesis 25:29-34

To put this in a context that is more contemporary, imagine that your sibling who is a successful surgeon came over to your house and said "(Insert your name here), I am sooo hungry! Please give me some of that chicken that you just fried and I will give you my practice, my 401(k), my IRA's, all of the heirloom jewelry that our parents willed to me and this winning lottery ticket. Would you take that deal? Would you make that deal? Esau is one of the clearest biblical examples of a person who did not understand their purpose in life, or how much they were valued. The scripture tells us Esau was weary. In other words, he was physically and mentally tired, *impatient* and exhausted. He traded something of a very high value, which was bestowed upon him – he didn't even have to do anything to earn it - and which would have ensured his position in the community and his prosperity, as well as that of his children for generations to come, for something that was of a comparatively low value. This is a clear example of someone who is out of control and being ruled by his own fleshy desires, and makes the case for fasting more. Denying the flesh and deliberately building our spiritual relationship with Christ during times of weariness and impatience can put us in position to be able to withstand any temptation. Esau put his spirit in jail and allowed his flesh to post bail. He made a permanent decision in a temporary state of mind. I declare to you right now and forever that you will NEVER make an Esau decision again in your life, in Jesus' name! From this day forward you will never make a major decision without first seeking the face of God! Fasting, praying and seeking God's direction on matters are strategies and tactics that you must use in order to counter the strategies and tactics that the devil uses to try and trick you out of what is rightfully yours. Many Christians are dying spiritually on a daily basis because of a lack of applied knowledge and understanding. Many of us know the Word, but we don't apply it because we don't know who we really are in Christ Jesus. You have been given the birthright, my friend. When God breathed the Breath of Life in you and made you a Speaking Spirit, just like He is, He then bestowed upon you all power and dominion in this earth. You have a legacy that ensures your place in the community and guarantees you prosperity in this world. God has given you a purpose, which you are to fulfill through various assignments, as part of an overall vision. Believe that and be 100% Spirit lead. Now is not the time or season for you to negotiate with the devil. Anything that he has to offer you is only temporary and belongs to you by your birthright anyway! It is your kingdom responsibility to know your covenant rights. My God! I am excited because I understand "Who I am and Whose I Am." Open your mouth and say *"I am a child of the Most High God. Hallelujah!"*

Do you believe that God is shifting things in your life right now? Even as you read this book? If you believe that, then decree and declare the following confessions with boldness and authority – out loud!

Open your mouth and say:

> *I am a valuable instrument to the kingdom of*
> *God!*
> *I was created with a purpose!*
> *I walk in my kingdom authority; Therefore no*
> *matter what I have gone through, I will not*
> *give up, Because God is on my side!*
> *I make a decision today to WIN!*
> *I make a decision to live life to the fullest!*
> *I make a decision to come out of my hiding*
> *place and walk into my dwelling place!*
> *God is speaking to me concerning my*
> *assignment right now!*
> *I proclaim today that I have victory in every*
> *area of my life. My life is ruled and governed*
> *by God.*
> *The devil is defeated! He has no power or*
> *control over me!*

Hallelujah, Hallelujah, and Hallelujah! If you believe that you ought to give God a crazy praise right now! Just thank Him for answering your prayers! Praise Him in advance for what He is about to do! You have so much inside of you. Don't give up! Someone needs to hear your testimony so that they won't give up. You can give out but never give up.

And we know that all things work together for good to them that love
God, to them who are the called according to his purpose.
Romans 8:28

As we conclude this chapter, remember that ALL things work together for good to them that love God. Do you love Him? If your answer is yes, then it will work out. That is good news! Every trial, every test, every tribulation, every hurt, every pain, and your past are going to work together for your good. You are the called according to God's purpose. No matter what you are seeing right now, it is working together for your good. The doctors may have given you some challenging news, but open your mouth and declare that "It is working together for my good!" You have the birthright! God has ordained a double portion just for you. You have prayed, you have waited and now it's your season to see the manifestation of everything you have believed God for. You just have to have enough faith to open your mouth and declare it! See yourself carrying out your purpose. See the vision that God has trusted you with. See yourself carrying out your assignments. See yourself prospering even as your soul prospers. See yourself free from the bondage of debt. See yourself healed and set free. See yourself overcoming. SEE YOUR SELF VICTORIOUS! It's working out for your good. Hallelujah!

You are a Victorious Individual of Purpose!

Chapter 2

Purging
"The Cleanse"

My God! You may as well go ahead and give God praise right now for what He has already done and for what He is going to do in your life! God is going to bless you beyond measure! You are going to burst at the seams because of the revelation that you are going to receive after reading this chapter! It is time for you to stop crying and to start praising God for the next level of worship, power and anointing. The chains that once kept you in bondage in your mind are being loosed and destroyed in the name of Jesus! Hallelujah! No more hold ups, setbacks or back seat living. God is the pilot of your life and the anchor of your soul. Are you ready for the next level? Walk into the newness of God, the freshness of God and the boldness of God. Hallelujah!

And be not conformed to this world: but be ye transformed by the renewing of your mind, that ye may prove what [is] that good, and acceptable, and perfect, will of God.
Romans 12:2

The word *transformed* means to change in nature and character. When your mind is renewed, your conversation changes; you stop living in the past and embrace the present, while thanking God for your future. When your mind is renewed, you realize that in spite of what happened

to you, God's grace and mercy has, and will always, carry you through. The grace and mercy of Jesus has keeping power. When your mind is renewed you prove to God what is good and acceptable. Not only does the Word of God have power, but you, too, have power!

In the previous chapter I talked about purpose and not giving up, because you were created for a reason. You exist to fulfill *your* purpose in life. In this chapter, though, I am going to deal with the mind. I want you to understand exactly what you are thinking and why you think the way that you do. Now let's look at the definition of the word purge.

Purge: verb (used with object)

1   to rid of whatever is impure or undesirable; cleanse; purify;
2   to rid, clear, or free (usually followed by of or from);
3   to clear of imputed guilt or ritual uncleanliness;
4   to clear away or wipe out legally (an offense, accusation, etc.) by atonement or other suitable action;
5   to remove by cleansing or purifying (often followed by away, off, or out)

Notice first that the word *purge* is a verb. That means that it is an action word and you will have to *do* something. Consider these questions: how do you really see yourself? Do you know what God says about you? Do you know who you are? Can you think of any reason why you should not be blessed by God? I want you to keep these questions in mind as you read through this chapter.

The thief does not come except to steal, and to kill, and to destroy.
I have come that they may have life, and that
they may have it more abundantly.
John 10:10

If the truth be told, there is no more time to waste! You must get on track to fulfill your assignment in the earth. You may be asking, "Lakeisha, why now?" My response to you is, "The devil is not after your things, he is after your mind, your character, your integrity, your faith, your vision and the Word of God that's on the inside of you." The time is now to renew your mind! Not tomorrow, not next week and not next year. But NOW! It is God's desire for you to live a life that is richly supplied, overflowing, and full of life. Are you ready to cleanse your mind and purge your spirit?

And do not be conformed to this world, but be transformed by the renewing of your mind, that you may prove what is that good, and acceptable, and perfect, will of God
Romans 12:2

The mind is a powerful thing. It deals with your understanding, your ability to reason, your feelings, thoughts and concentration. It also has the capacity to store tons of useful and useless information, knowledge and memories. It holds the good, the bad and the ugly for you. There will be seasons in your life, when you must have a mental purging. Just as it is healthy to cleanse your colon every three to six months, so too, must your mind be cleansed and purged. Over the years, you may have downloaded so much junk into the hard drive of your mind that it is literally affecting the way that you live, think, speak and react. The hard drive of your mind can become infected with viruses that need to be wiped out. In other words, you *need* to be purged of some memories. Not archived and put away for another time, but deleted, emptied out and totally eliminated!

My vision for this chapter is to deal with you and any underlying issue that needs to be confronted and placed on the table about the way you think and believe. You might not even know what to think of yourself because of some of the information that *your mind* has received about *you* from other people. Your family, friends, and past relationships have played a part in your thinking process. It is time, though, for you to tap into who you *really* are. In case you didn't know it, let me first declare to you that *YOU* are powerful, boldly anointed, and valuable! The devil knows that once you begin to believe this for yourself, you will no longer be defeated. There is nothing that you won't be able to do with the Holy Spirit guiding you. So, I ask you today: whose reports are you going to believe; those of man or of the Lord?

The question is, are you ready to kiss your past goodbye and learn who you really are? Are you ready to see a move of God in your life, in your mind and in your heart? The time is now to rebuild, reclaim and redirect your life and mind to the Father. ***Who are you?*** You are a child of the living God, predestined for greatness before the foundations of this world! And that is just the beginning of the good news!

> *"And those he predestined, he also called; those he called, he also justified; those he justified, he also glorified.*
> ***Romans 8:30***

WOW! What I love about this scripture is the word *predestined*, which means to be determined in advance. What an awesome God! Before you were even born, God already knew every detail of your life, what you would do and what you would not do. He knew when and how you would rebel all while you were still in your mother's womb. Yet, He still called you to do His works. Then, He justified you, meaning that you are blameless and innocent in spite of the things that you did that were not pleasing in His sight. Now I want you to really get the revelation in what I am about to tell you. Because you are blameless before Him, the Almighty God also praises you! My God! I rejoice off that alone, knowing that I can praise God with all I have and in return, my Father will do the same for me. That is overwhelming and humbling and simply amazing! That's the type of God we serve. He is so giving and so full of life. God is a selfless God.

When I was a little girl, I used to express my feelings, thoughts, emotions and fears on paper. Writing was, and still is, my outlet. My thoughts on paper are my voice, my expression, my silent and loud cry. My mind could have become a stained canvas because of some of the things I have experienced and seen; the good, the bad and the ugly. However, the total picture is so beautiful that it is actually a priceless work of art. No one will ever be able to pay me for the painting that I painted because it was created for me to become the woman that God intended for me to become.

One day while I was driving, I heard a pastor say "Who Are You?" This is a simple question, the answer to which most of us can easily rattle off – I am a woman, a sister, a daughter, a friend, a professional, etc. However, on this day, that question seemed profound to me, and stopped me in my mental tracks. I felt confused. Then, I asked myself "Who Are You, Lakeisha?" It is one thing to know what God says about you but it's another thing entirely to understand what you truly believe about yourself. My mind raced and was flooded with thoughts, so I immediately pulled over to the side of the road and began to write what I thought.

> *"I, Lakeisha Dixon am a woman of power who walks in the anointing of God; a woman who is blessed and highly favored, a wise Proverbs 31 woman. I am a rich and wealthy woman. I am a woman with the heart and mind of Christ. I am a woman that will bring thousands of souls to Christ through the teaching of the Good News of the Gospel. I am a woman who carries the weight of the world on her shoulders (which happens when you don't cast your cares on the Father). I am a woman who deals with low self-esteem, which causes me to emotionally over eat, while faced with the issues of trust and rejection."*

Now as you can see, I started off positive, and then the more I wrote, I began to express how I really felt about who I was. What I wrote in the beginning was what I wanted to be and where I knew God would eventually take me. On the surface, that is what I believed, but when I started to dig, I got down to my own beliefs. Unfortunately, though, that is where most people stop. Thank God for deliverance! I understood that if I kept digging that I would eventually reach the root, and that is what I needed to do if I was to be truly purged of those things that did not belong to me. I had been through so many negative things in my life that I had begun to believe them about myself! The root of my negative thinking had come from my negative life experiences. As I continued to write, I started to understand that I had shaped my own belief system through pain, disappointments, fear and hurt. My mind was tainted and my words were bitter and angry. I asked myself again "WHO AM I?!", and then I continued to write. This process for me was the first step towards my deliverance.

What I learned is that I could fool myself and others but I couldn't fool God! The devil didn't care about me nor anything that concerned me; his goal was to try to get me to take my eyes off of God and to focus on me and my situation. He knew he would have won if he could have kept me from seeing myself the way that God saw me.

So God created man in his own image, in the image of God He
created him; male and female He created them.
Genesis 1:27

He beat on my mind and thoughts like a drum and I listened to that foolishness, until I processed that negativity in my spirit. However, I finally came to the conclusion that what I really needed was a better perception of myself, because no matter what God said about me, if I didn't believe it, I would never be able to conceive who I really am in Christ. I learned that if I did not deal with the issues that formed my negative thoughts and way of thinking then I would always see myself through scaly eyes, never really sure of what I was actually looking at. Once the scales were removed I was able to see myself in the image and likeness of God. The enemy came in to try to steal my joy, kill my spirit and to destroy my life, and he used the people around me to do it. But it really didn't matter what people may have said, done or thought about me because I was created in the image of God! I learned that an idle mind is the devil's playground so I had to stop giving the enemy room to get God's glory.

And if children, then heirs; heirs of God, and joint-heirs with Christ;
if so be that we suffer with [him], that we may be also
glorified together.
Romans 8:17

As humans, we are all born with the same bloodline as our parents, but as believers, we are now under the bloodline of Christ. In Christ we are victorious and we win because of the blood that was shed for the remission of our sins. God paid the ultimate price so that we may have abundant lives! You, my friend, are a child of the living God! Knowing who you are will make you a better vessel for the Kingdom of God and less vulnerable to Satan's plan.

You can't bring back the past. It is gone. You can't change it; you can't go back and re-live it. All you have is today and the possibilities of tomorrow. You have a whole future and a destiny ahead of you. I know that it hurts. I know that they abused you and lied on you. Some have even tried to sabotage your name but you have to walk in forgiveness. Forgiveness is the tool that God uses to help you to move on and move forward. You are to walk in forgiveness so that you can have peace that surpasses understanding and a sound mind. You cannot respond to your past because it will keep you in bondage and keep your mind in prison. The time is now for you to be free from past hurts and pain.

> *For if ye forgive men their trespasses,*
> *your heavenly Father will also forgive you.*
> **Matthew 6:14**

Allow God to breathe His Spirit into you. Leave the past in the past. Right now you may be so stuck in your past that you can't even see the blessings that God has prepared and placed right in front of you. God is saying, "Let go! Your blessings are ahead of you, not behind you. The past is what's keeping you in bondage, Let it go." God is opening the prison gates of your mind right now. We all have been hurt. Some of us have been in situations where we have hurt people who we love. Some of us were hurt by people who were supposed to love and protect us. However, we must move on from it, move on past it, and most importantly, just move on! So when God says "let go", you'd better let go. Don't look back. Lay it to rest and move forward. I once read this quote by Dr. Mike Murdock: "Never stay in a place where you are tolerated and not celebrated." If someone does not recognize your worth or your value, then you would be doing yourself a favor when you throw your own going away party and leave! Whatever you do... *DON'T LOOK BACK*! Even when they ask you where you are going!

God wants to restore you. The more you hold on to it, the more that individual or thing has power and authority over you. Forgive so that yokes can be removed and burdens can be destroyed off of your life. It's time to love again, to breathe again, to laugh again, to embrace again and to live again. The bible declares that you shall have peace and you shall enjoy the fruits of your labor. Walk in your God-given

authority. YOU HAVE POWER and DOMINION! Now it's time to walk in it.

> *Good and upright [is] the LORD:*
> *therefore will he teach sinners in the way.*
> **Psalm 25:8**

When you have no foundation in Christ, You are just like a mouse in a maze. You'll never find your way out because God isn't your source and isn't guiding your direction. One of the benefits of knowing Him is that He will make a way out of no way for you. Below you will find some practical things that I did in order to see myself through the eyes of God.

First, I prayed and asked God to give me a better image of myself. I asked Him to help me to see the value that He sees in me, to understand the joy that He feels when He looks at me, and the love that He had for me when He died on the cross of Calvary. I wanted to see myself the way God sees me. I also prayed that God would strip off and eliminate some things from the hard drive of my mind that had been stopping me from becoming all that I was created to be. I developed a passion and a thirst for praying. I woke up speaking the Word of God. I went to sleep speaking the Word of God. I began declaring and confessing words of wisdom, power and strength over my life. I watered myself daily with the Word of God.

> *But what saith it? The word is nigh thee, [even] in thy mouth, and in*
> *thy heart: that is, the word of faith, which we preach.*
> **Romans 10:8**

Deliverance and change is a process. You have to decide to open your mouth and declare some great things about yourself. God has already said it, so why can't you? If you want to reap the rewards of going to your job every day, you have to decide whether to stay in bed or to get up and go, regardless of how you feel, right? The decisions that you make can either press life out of you or push you into greatness. After I came to understand that, changing my life was as simple as making the decision to change my mind. I noticed right away that I was able to receive a compliment without countering it with something negative. Instead, I learned to simply say "Thank You."

"This Book of the Law shall not depart from your mouth, but you shall meditate in it day and night, that you may observe to do according to all that is written in it. For then you will make your way prosperous, and then you will have good success."
Joshua 1:8

This is so powerful to me because it clearly states that the word of God should not depart from your mouth, which means that you should only declare the same things that God has already said. This means that the word of God should be an active part of your conversation, buried in your thoughts, replayed in your ears, engraved in your heart, and evident in your walk with Christ. You should always think about the Good News of the Gospel and apply it to your everyday life. Once you follow instructions and walk in obedience, you will flourish in the things of God with good fortune and success. God will make sure you are well off.

And they overcame him by the blood of the Lamb, and by the word of their testimony.
Revelations 12:11(a)

Therefore, I challenge you today to use the space provided below and answer the question, "Who Are You?" Be honest with yourself about how you see yourself. Remember, this chapter is about purging, which is one of the first steps to cleansing. Do not judge yourself by only writing what you think you *should* write; but write what's in your heart, positive and negative, who you believe you are at this very moment in time. Let God be God alone. If you need more space, use another sheet of paper. This exercise is THAT important!

"I,_____(your name), am

_____

_____

_____

_____

_____

_____

_____

_____

_____

_____

_____

_____

_____

_____

_____

_____

_____

_____

_____

_____

_____

_____

_____

_____

_____

_____

_____

_____

_____

_____

_____."

Now that you have finished writing, take a moment to reflect on what you wrote. Give yourself permission to feel what you feel about what you wrote. Now, positive or negative, give all of what you wrote over to God! Now write down some of the things you aim to change in your life. This is going to help you to become the best person God has created you to be. DO NOT make the mistake of beating yourself up if you are not able to accomplish all of your goals. Remember, God has already declared you victorious! Believe and accept that fact!

Fear thou not; for I [am] with thee: be not dismayed; for I [am] thy God: I will strengthen thee; yea, I will help thee; yea, I will uphold thee with the right hand of my righteousness.
Isaiah 41:10

Some practical steps that you can take to increase your chances of reaching your goals are:

1   Set short and long term goals for yourself
2   Visit your goals at least once a week
3   Check off steps to completion of each goal and cross them off as you complete them
4   Revisit and revise your goals as necessary

When this is done, you will begin to live a more fulfilled life knowing that if God be for you then no one can stand against you. This may not be easy, but God will be there to guide you and lead you into all truth, understanding and revelation with His WORD. I believe in you. You are victorious!

I can do all things through Christ which strengtheneth me.
Phillipians 4:13

This scripture says **_all_** things! Not some or most things, but all things! Make a righteous resolve to think outside the box, live in total reverence to God and to speak life **only** over your situations, no matter what they look like. Water you mind daily with the Word of God.

Going back to my previous example, what do you think would have

happened had I not opened my own mouth and declared that I was healed from Psoriasis? What if I had just believed the doctor's report for my life? I wouldn't be walking in my healing right now! I would have missed out on something that is rightfully mine. Even in my weakest moments, I confessed that I was healed from the crown of my head to the soles of my feet. I continued to confess that God was healing me now, despite what I saw or felt. I had to make a decision to take control of my mind before it took control of me. You have to do the same thing right now. Speak greatness over your own life. If you don't, who will?

So then faith comes by hearing and hearing by the word of God.
Romans 10:17

Read the Word out loud, speak the Word to yourself or listen to the Word of God when it is preached or read. There is always fresh excitement and a fresh revelation in hearing the Word of God. You do your part and God will do the rest. Faith is the key to God's heart. God has chosen you and He wants you walking in VICTORY!!! What the devil meant for evil God has made to work together for your good. Your mind has to be renewed so that you won't continue to do the same things you used to do. Think about all the times you thought you were not going to make it and God showed up and showed out in your life and it blew your mind. Your family and friends thought you wouldn't be able to make it out of that one. Just think about the messes that you have been in and start praising our Redeemer right now for bringing you all the way through. Hallelujah! When God wants to bless you, He does not need your history report. All He wants to know is do you want to be made whole. Consider the story of the man who had been lame for 38 years.

After this there was a feast of the Jews; and Jesus went up to Jerusalem. Now there is in Jerusalem by the sheep market a pool, which is called in the Hebrew tongue Bethesda, having five porches. In these lay a great multitude of impotent folk, of blind, halt, withered, waiting for the moving of the water. For an angel went down at a certain season into the pool, and troubled the water: whosoever then first after the troubling of the water stepped in was

made whole of whatsoever disease he had. And a certain man was there, which had an infirmity thirty and eight years. When Jesus saw him lie, and knew that he had been now a long time in that case, he saith unto him, Wilt thou be made whole? The impotent man answered him, Sir, I have no man, when the water is troubled, to put me into the pool: but while I am coming, another steppeth down before me. Jesus saith unto him, Rise, take up thy bed, and walk. And immediately the man was made whole, and took up his bed, and walked: and on the same day was the Sabbath."-
John 5:1-12

My God! Every time I read this story, my soul gets excited because this is clearly an example of what can happen when God shows up. This man had had an infirmity for 38 years. In others words, he was weak, sick, impotent, defeated and affected. That's a long time to be suffering. However, Jesus showed up and asked the man "Wilt thou be made whole?" This man began to talk about what happened in the past. Again, you have got to let go of past. Jesus doesn't need the permission of your past to bless you *right now*! That's the Word of the Lord for you right now, "Rise up, take up your bed and walk!" In other words, take up those issues that you have made your resting place - your burdens, your place of contentment and complacency - and walk. Jesus is a Master problem solver. You must understand that there is nothing that is too hard for God. You must position yourself to receive from God when He shows up. "Do you want to be made whole?" God wants to bless you. Don't be so busy giving Him your history reports that you are not able to have an ear to hear what the Spirit of the Lord is saying to you.

But thou [art] holy, [O thou] that inhabits the praises of Israel.
Psalm 22:3

I would be in error if I didn't reveal to you a key component of activating your faith and keeping up your spiritual strength while you are going through this period of purging in the Lord. It is worship. Gospel recording artist Wess Morgan has a song entitled "I choose to worship." I played this song for over an hour and everything about this song is a declaration and confession. My spirit rejoiced and shouted in victory as I began singing the words:

> *"I choose to worship*
> *My mind is made up*
> *I just can't give up.*
> *He's healing me*
> *I'm going to worship."*

That lets me know that worship is the key to deliverance and restoration. You just can't remain the same when you are glorifying God. He's sovereign in all His ways. He's faithful. He's worthy of all the glory, praise and honor. I had to let you know that no matter what it looks like now, God is able to heal your past and launch you into your destiny. Just worship the King of Kings, the Prince of Peace, the Rock of Your Salvation, the Creator of Heaven and Earth. The Alpha and Omega, Your Beginning and Your Ending! God is a Present Help in a time of trouble! He is the Lifter of Your head! God is changing you, He's healing you, He's delivering you, and He sent the Holy Spirit to pray and intercede for you. God will keep your mind and your spirit in perfect peace. Just worship Him! Hallelujah!

You are an Individual of Purging!

Chapter 3

Passion
"The Desire"

Wow, my spirit is already ignited! I am pumped up, fired up and ready to go - and this is only the third chapter! Let me just say this, "Ain't nobody mad but the devil." You should be excited to know that your life is changing for the better. Whatever you are seeing now is still not God's best for you. There is still so much more that God desires to show you. He wants to reveal to you all the plans that He has for your life. Can you imagine the people who are waiting to meet you? Have you ever met someone for the first time and found out that you were able to encourage them? It may have been something as simple as a compliment, a smile, a listening ear or just a simple word. Someone is waiting on you to bless them. Bless means "to make whole; to empower". God has placed something on the inside of you that is so immensely powerful and, when activated, can change your whole world and save your household. You are a chosen vessel and God wants to use you. I don't know about you but I want to be in position for God to use me. I want to make sure I am walking and operating in my divine assignment according to the will of God.

It is time for your spiritual eyes to be opened to righteousness, awakened to vision and submitted to passion. The more you know, the more you will grow and develop in your kingdom assignment. Your

purpose for living is tied very closely to your passion. This passion is not to be confused with the lustful or sinful "passion" of the world, but it is a desire to provoke ambition in your life and to cause change in someone else's life. It is a deep seated desire to live for God and be in His presence. It is a longing to move mountains and to see the yoke destroying power of Jesus being made manifest in the earth. What have you been called, created, and designed to do? Once you tap into that very thing that you love to do, you will not become easily moved, swayed or frustrated while doing it. We must look to God for guidance and directions. We cannot lean on the opinions of others. We must lean and trust in our Lord. We all have been called to do something.

Trust in the Lord with all your heart and lean not on your own understanding. In all your ways acknowledge Him, and He will make your paths straight.
Proverbs 3:5

The dictionary defines passion as "any powerful or compelling emotion or feeling; strong, amorous feeling or desire; love, ardor, or the object of such a fondness or desire; enthusiasm or desire for anything. Passion is a burning desire to do something with love, emotion and feeling. I did not discover my passion right away. I just enjoyed listening and talking to people about their problems. So much so that in elementary school, I use to get in trouble because I was always talking and getting out of my seat to help the other kids. I was also a giver; I would go to school and give out all my hair bows to the little girls who did not have any. My mom would get so upset with me because no matter how much she disciplined me, I still went to school giving my hair bows away. I can laugh now but my mom was not laughing. I remember sharing my lunch money with other students just to make sure they had something to eat. God was positioning me at a young age to do His will. He was grooming me in elementary school. He was developing me at that age to become the woman that He purposed me to be. We must recognize the gifting and talents in our children when they are young and encourage and nurture them in their passions.

I was such a nurturing child that by the time I reached high school my nickname was "Mama." My friends, and even strangers, were calling me Mama. I knew that I had a caring and compassionate heart. God has given us all a gift but it is up to us to use it. I began to notice that I was truly set apart. I was different from other students who were my age. For one thing, I was a lot more mature, which was probably because I was babysitting my baby sister while my mom and stepdad worked late night shifts. I "played the part" so often that at times, I felt like *I* was a teenage mom.

Now, I've already told you that both of my Grannies made sure that I was skilled in the things of God; however, as I continued to grow and mature physically, I began to receive spiritual guidance and instruction from people outside of my immediate family, too. My friend Hasina's mother, Mrs. Williams, exposed me to fasting as a lifestyle while I was in high school. Through my dedication and elevations through discipline, which is one of the many benefits of fasting, I began to burn even hotter for the things of God.   I joined the bible club at my school, which brought us to the school a half an hour early to pray around the flagpole, touching and agreeing for the safety of the other students, faculty, staff and any visitors to the school. We were a powerful club because we were taught by other students, how to live a holy and purified life for Christ, even as teens.

My passion for people and helping others continued to grow. My desire to demonstrate love to other people became so strong that I would go out of my way to give compliments, provoke conversation with strangers and pray for my family and friends on a daily bases. It broke my heart to see people hurting, frustrated, broken and spiritually confused. I wanted to heal the hearts of God's people. This passion – this burning desire, filled my heart and led me to really commit to doing the work of the Lord.

One of my spiritual fathers, Pastor Cecil Lamb, at Spirit of Christ Center and Ministries, taught me that the very thing that I have a passion to do somehow lines up with my calling. At that very moment I knew I was called to be an evangelist. I eventually became ordained as an evangelist under the leadership of Pastor Lamb and the Fisher of Men Development Institute. The desire to minister to and to help

people was so rooted inside of me that it always seemed like I was always on the verge of bursting at the seams to tell people about the goodness of Jesus. I was laying hands on the sick, confused and lost. I have seen miracles take place through my passion and my steadfast faith. I remember tapping into the power of ministering to people everywhere, in the stores, malls, nail and hair salons, and on my job. When an opportunity presented itself, I told anyone who would listen something about Jesus! It's funny now thinking back on it. I was so young and so eager to please the Lord. It really was like fire shut up in my bones! I was so on fire to be in His will.

> *Delight yourself in the Lord and He will give you*
> *the desires of your heart.*
> ***Psalms 37:4***

One thing I know for sure is that God is not a liar. If He said it, then it shall come to pass. God will give you the desires of your heart. Not only that but He also planted inside of you the resources and tools that you will need to minister effectively. It is time for you to be at a place in your life where you want to take ownership and responsibility for your life, stop playing the role of the victim, and began to help others heal. You will find deliverance for yourself in helping someone else to be delivered. Once you hear someone else's testimony you will realize that your situation is not as bad as you thought.

It's time for Believers to make an impact in the lives of family, friends, churches and communities. You have been called to impact the nations. God has already set you apart for greatness. You have an assignment and the devil is trying to stop your testimony from being heard, but I declare to you right now, that in the name of Jesus, you will fulfill your purpose! You may have step back in order to move forward, but praise God anyway because when He is involved, a setback is a setup for the ultimate comeback! Hallelujah! You have an assignment and it is your responsibility to bring your vision into fruition. When you are operating from the position for which God has created you then you are aligned with the Spirit of the Lord. You then have access to God's "super" to cover and replace your "natural" and you become a supernatural individual.

"But you will receive power when the Holy Spirit comes on you"
Acts 1:8

Many people are not fulfilled in their callings because they are operating with no POWER, having only a form of godliness. Don't find yourself in the unfortunate position of laboring under your call but lacking in the power that can only come from God's Holy Spirit. You can never fulfill your assignment without the help of the Holy Spirit. The Bible says He is your Comforter, Advocate, Power and your Intercessor. You want the help of the Holy Spirit because He is our spiritual point of contact to access the supernatural power of God. His help allows you to go and to press much further than where you are able to go and what you are able to do on your own. Your passions should burn so deeply inside of you that even if you tried, you could never shake it off. You should wake up thinking about your passion and you should fall asleep thinking about your passion.

And seeing a fig tree afar off having leaves, he came, if haply he might find anything thereon: and when he came to it, he found nothing but leaves; for the time of figs was not [yet].
Mark 11:13

If you look around, you will discover that so many people are not happy in many areas of their lives because they are not living up to their full potential. I feel bad for these people because they are not living out their passions. They are simply going through the motions of everyday life, completing routine tasks and assignments, and literally toiling and laboring. They are not being what they were created to be, and they are not doing what they were created to do. For example, a fish was created to be a fish. It was designed to live in water. They were designed to take oxygen directly from the water they live in into their blood stream and release carbon dioxide back into the water they expel. If you take a living fish out of its natural habitat and put in a tank of air, this critical gas exchange cannot happen, and the fish will eventually die, because a fish cannot take oxygen from the air. You can pour water over it to try to give it oxygen, but unless it is submerged and moving, it will die. Now, let's apply that same logic to the spiritual realm. If a person is taken out of his or her spiritual habitat

through prayerlessness, disobedience, unrepentant sin, etc., then the Holy Spirit cannot stay, and he or she won't be able to live holy for very long off of someone occasionally splashing bits of the Word on them. This is known as a spiritual death; but thanks be to God for the resurrecting power of Jesus!

Trust in the LORD with all your heart, and lean not on your own understanding; in all your ways acknowledge Him, and He shall direct your paths.
Proverbs 3:5-6

God will give you instructions on what to do and where to go; however, if you don't know what He is talking about and you decide to follow your own GPS system instead of His, then you take matters into your own hands and end up carrying your burden on your own, and detouring from the path that He made straight for you. As a result of your own disobedience you will find yourself on Set Back Street, Frustrated Avenue and Pity Party Lane. Don't let this happen to you and if it does, then don't blame God for not showing up! He has given you His Word as your guide but if you keep ignoring His instruction, then the fault, error and blame, are all on you. God is your source and you must stay connected to the one who is giving you power. You were created to soar like an eagle, to eat the best, live in the best and to walk in dominion and power.

You must trust God. In other words, your reliance, strength and ability all lie with and in God. The question here is "Do you trust God to direct your paths? Because once you get a revelation on what you have been created to do, then God is going to show up and show out on your behalf. Hallelujah! What is that passion that has been burning inside of you? God is asking, "Do you trust Me to bring it to fruition?" You may as well start shouting, dancing and praising now, knowing that you are getting ready to tap into a whole new dimension of your life!

Once, when a business opportunity was presented to me, the first thing I asked myself is "How is my new career and business venture going to allow me to continue to fulfill my passion for doing what God has created me to do?" I had to remember that God does send vehicles to get you to your destination. See, I almost missed it because I was thinking about the four walls of the church, not yet remembering that *I* am the church! So are you. We are all one body in Christ Jesus. I had to remember that God would send men and women from all different backgrounds to hear the good news of the Gospel. They would be hurt, broken and abused despite any money that they were making. God reminded me that hearts still needed to be healed and that minds still needed to be regulated and renewed. God used me in corporate settings to pray, heal and deliver. I learned that I did not have to dilute my faith and confidence in God just because another individual was lost, because I had the power on my life to minster and share the word of God.

It may surprise you to know, but God will use you right where you are, even in your work place. I know this to be true because He used me, and He may desire to use you, too. I was working for a large corporation when one day my boss called me out of the blue to come into her office to pray for her. This was when I realized that God will set some things up in the spirit realm that will blow your mind. It is not common practice for employers to call on employees for such personal and intimate contact, particularly not in our culture of litigation and lawsuits. I finally got the revelation of why prayer warriors and intercessors have to always be prepared, ready and equipped to pray and minister the word of God at any given time. This encounter reinforced what I learned as I was coming up in the church, which is that people are watching the way you carry yourself as a Christian. Sometimes, you are the only Bible that a person will see. My boss at the time knew that I was a born again believer and she could see that I walked the walk and that my walk lined up with my talk. This encounter also taught me that no matter what position, title or number is in your bank account, we all need God! This woman knew that I was a woman of excellence based on my work ethic and she also knew that I knew God. I'm going to ask you a provocative question right now. What examples are you setting in your work place? Is your faith an open secret, or does everyone know that they can count on you to get a prayer through?

Whether you realize it or believe it, or not, God has given you a

platform to touch hearts, change minds and save souls all across the nations. All because of that passion that Christ placed on the inside of you that burns deep in your heart. What is burning on the inside of you? What situations are you seeing that break your heart and make your cry? What has captivated your attention and won't let you stop thinking about it? These questions will guide you toward what you are supposed to be doing. They will help you to identify your passion.

And he bearing his cross went forth into a place called [the place] of a skull, which is called in the Hebrew Golgotha: Where they crucified him, and two others with him, on either side one, and Jesus in the midst.
John 19:17-18

"Surely He has borne our griefs and carried our sorrows; yet we esteemed Him stricken, Smitten by God, and afflicted. But He was wounded for our transgressions, He was bruised for our iniquities; the chastisement for our peace was upon Him, and by His stripes we are healed."
Isaiah 53:4-5

When I think of passion, I think of the price Jesus had to pay for our lives. He was beaten, bruised, assaulted, spat upon, pierced, hung and left to die so that we may live. It amazes me that Jesus put us ahead of Himself. He could have run, hid, cursed and even lied to stop from dying and being afflicted with pain. However, He saw the problems, He saw the sin, and He saw the greatest gift. He saw love. He saw us. Jesus was, and still is, a Master problem-solver. He knew that His assignment was greater than Himself.

Use the space below to answer the following questions. Remember, this is personal for you and the same rules apply. Be honest with yourself, don't beat yourself up and let God be God alone.

What am I afraid of?
Am I operating in my full potential now?
What is that thing God has created me to do that I can't or won't do?
What's holding me back?
Am I ready to walk into a new season of life where God is in full control?

_____

_____

_____

_____

_____

_____

_____

_____

_____

_____

_____

_____

These questions will help you get to where you need to be and become the person God created the world to see. Don't look at the now but instead look at the possibilities of your future. You were created for the Glory of God. You were created to win. You were created with passion. You were called to do the will of the Father.

You are an Individual of Passion!

Chapter 4

Prayer
"The Power"

PRAISE BREAK!!! Let's give God the praise!! Allow me to remind you that He is worthy of all the Glory and the Honor! He is the Author and Finisher of your faith! He is a present help in times of trouble! He is the Lily of the Valley! He is the Messiah! He is your Savior! He is a keeping God! He is a Consuming Fire! He is the Chief Cornerstone! He is All Knowing and All Powerful! He is the lifter of your soul! He is your Advocate! He is the Word! He is a Sovereign! He is your Rock and your Fortress! He is your way maker and your deliver! He is God! Hallelujah!!!

The steps of a good man are ordered by the LORD, And He delights in his way. Though he fall, he shall not be utterly cast down; For the LORD upholds him with His hand. I have been young, and now am old; yet I have not seen the righteous forsaken,
nor his descendants begging bread.
Psalm 37:23-25

The Bible says that we are to enter into His courts with praise and into His gates with thanksgiving! So, we ought to praise Him! He's the lamp under your feet that lights your pathway! He is Jehovah Jireh, the God that provides! He is Jehovah Nissi, our banner and our victory! He

is Jehovah Rapha, the God who heals! Every muscle, tissue, fiber, organ and cell in your body must line up according to the will of the Father! He is Jehovah Shammah, the God who is always there! He will never leave you nor forsake you! He is the pilot of your life and the captain of your destiny! He is the substance of our very being! He is the Great "I Am"! Call Him Jesus! Hallelujah! Hallelujah! Hallelujah!

Now let's talk about prayer! Let's experience another level of God's glory and grace upon our lives!

> *The effectual fervent prayer of a righteous man availeth much.*
> ***James 5:16(b)***

Prayer is defined as a reverent petition made to God; an act of communion with God; a worship; devotion; a confession or praise; thanksgiving; adoration; a fervent request; appreciation; revelation; dedication; elevation; activation. Simply put, prayer is your conversation with God. If there was a formula for accessing God, then prayer would be the "active" ingredient. It is the key that turns the lock.

In order for prayers to be most effective, the act of praying has to become a lifestyle for you. Prayer is very personal, transparent and revealing. It is fellowship with the Father and it is also your lifeline to God. You must take time out every day to pray and humble yourself before the Lord. Prayer is my life. It is a lifestyle. Can you imagine being faced with something or someone harmful or dangerous and being rescued or getting relief in a split second just by shouting "Jesus!"? My God! The word says that if you pray according to His Will that He will hear from above, and if He hears, then you shall have your petition. It is God's desire for you to be safe, whole and blessed, and all of that is accessible to you through prayer!!! If Jesus had to take time to pray then you should know that it is only wise for you to have to pray.

Prayer is my life. I set aside a certain amount of time daily to converse and commune with the Father. This is where I draw my strength. My prayers, though, are not limited to my "prayer time". I remain connected through constant communication throughout my day. In addition to set prayer times, I talk to God all day about what I am, or should be, doing. I listen to God when He speaks back to me. Remember, this is a conversation. When you talk to God, He talks back. In the same way that you would talk to a trusted friend, advisor or parent, you can and should talk to God.

Just as there are different types of conversations, there are different types of prayers. For instance, if someone does something nice for you, you thank them for it, right? You may explain your gratitude with descriptive language or with great detail and sincerity. Well, when God does something nice for you and you talk to Him about it, using descriptive language and great detail and sincerity, then that is a prayer of thanksgiving. If you are feeling loving toward a parent, friend or spouse just because of who they have been in your life and you express it to them using words of sincerity and love, doesn't it make them feel happy and appreciated? Well, when you tell God how much you love and appreciate Him, that is a prayer of adoration, and if adoration warms the heart of your natural father, how much more would it warm the heart of your Heavenly Father?

Now, you must also take time to pray for your family, your friends, and your enemies; those who have hurt and wronged you. Believe it or not, it is actually easier than it sounds to pray for your enemies once you understand your purpose, go through your purging and are operating in your passion. You must also pray for lost souls, your businesses, your communities and the nations. I know, I know, sometimes we have to dig a little deeper to pray for those who have authority over us.

"And when He had sent the multitudes away, He went up on the mountain by Himself to pray. Now when evening came, He was alone there."
Matthew 14:23

While there is no part of your relationship with God that is "more important" than any other part, it is prayer, the words that you speak from your mouth, that activate the atmosphere around you. Even Jesus, our example in the earth, took time to pray. Remember, God made you

in His image, which refers to how you appear physically, and in His likeness, which refers to what you have the ability to do. God is a Spirit, so He made you a spirit. When God speaks, He is a Speaking Spirit, and whatever He says surely comes to pass. When you speak, you, too, are a speaking spirit, and whatever you say, shall come to pass. So, be very careful what words you unleash upon the world.

Jesus took time out to pray so that He would be in tune with the will of His Father in Heaven. Prayer builds strength. God answers your questions while you are in prayer; He sends you divine ideas and strategies while you are in prayer. The mysteries of the kingdom are revealed in prayer. Guidance and direction is also delivered while you are in prayer. When you pray, you are in direct communication with the Father. It's just you and God. You're communing with God and God, in return, is communing with you.

If my people, who are called by my name, will humble themselves and pray and seek my face and turn from their wicked ways, then will I hear from heaven and will forgive their sin and will heal their land.
2 Chronicles 7:14

This scripture is so powerful to me because it clearly states that if we humble ourselves, pray, seek and turn from our wicked ways, God will forgive our sin and heal our land. The word "heal" means: to make healthy again, to make sound, freed from evil, cleansed, purified, restored. God is saying He wants to cleanse you and restore you to your original form, the "you" that He created you to be, while giving you peace. If this is not enough to have you praising right now then you have missed it!

Land represents every dry thing and place in your life that needs to be healed, nurtured, restored and resurrected. So, whatever "land" you have in your life that needs to be healed today, God has given you clear instructions on how to see the manifestations of forgiveness and healing take place. Wow! Even if you have some stuff that you can't tell anybody about, guess what? You can tell God. He won't tell anyone else AND He can forgive it and heal it! Hallelujah! God can heal your land even when you are going through a season of drought!

44

In other words, when it seems that everything in your life is stagnant, dormant, inactive, or dead; when nothing is growing or producing or living, except for weeds and thorns, just one touch from God will transform that season into provision. Ask yourself, "What land do I need God to heal right now"?

I am reminded of a story of the woman with the issue of blood for 12 long years. Now whether male or female, can you imagine bleeding all day every day for 4,380 days? Whether it is blood or physical pain, wouldn't you use every resource in your power to find relief? Doctors, medicines, experimental treatments, specialists, surgeons, whatever it took to get your healing, right? Is there anything you would not do to try to fix the problem? Anything you wouldn't sell or give away if you thought it would help? This woman spent all she had to try to fix her issue, yet found no relief. No relief that is, until she pressed in and activated the healing power of prayer. The Bible records that **_she said within herself_** "if I could only touch the hem of His garment then I will be made whole." See, this tells me that you are going to have issues that no one will be able to fix except for Jesus, but you have to activate it by pressing in and speaking out! This story excites me, so I have to repeat it here in its entirety.

And, behold, a woman, which was diseased with an issue of blood twelve years, came behind [him], and touched the hem of his garment: For she said within herself, if I may but touch his garment, I shall be whole. But Jesus turned him about, and when he saw her, he said, Daughter, be of good comfort; thy faith hath made thee whole. And the woman was made whole from that hour.
Matthew 9:20-22

My God, My God! I can hardly contain myself as I write because not only was she bold, but she accessed her rights as a child of God, and a child of authority, and exercised her faith to activate the power. She made up in her mind that she was going to be healed that day and believed that Jesus would do it. There was a crowd of folks around Jesus but when you need something from the Master not even a devil in hell can stop you from getting God's attention. What excites me about this is He said, "Who touched ME? Glory to God! There is

something that you, the individual, can do to stop God in his tracks. Your praise, your worship and your reach has got to be so powerful that even in a crowd God can still feel your touch. Your worship has got to be so powerful that God stops and looks for you so that He can bless you. How desperate are you to get God's attention?

Let me tell you another story. I received a call that a friend needed help desperately because she was having major complications with the birth of her child. As an intercessor in our ministry, we normally receive prayer requests via email, so when I received a phone call instead I knew that this was immediate warfare. She had gone into labor prematurely, and while giving birth, the baby's heart stopped. She was immediately taken into surgery for an emergency cesarean. I began to pray and intercede because in addition to walking in my calling, this was personal. I know this the young lady personally, and because she is my friend, I was aware of some of the complications that she experienced while carrying her baby, too. I went to pick up another friend of ours, Kimmie, because I knew that she, too, was a woman of faith. (This is why you must be careful and deliberate in choosing your friends and associates. Hanging around the wrong sphere of influence can dilute your judgment and thinking, and can cause you to live and behave in ways that are not conducive to an environment of faith, which produces miracles, and a miracle is what we needed that night!)

> *For where two or three are gathered together in my name,*
> *there am I in the midst of them.*
> ***Matthew 18:20***

We reached the hospital two hours after she had given birth. She was so upset, as would any new mother whose child's life is threatened. She had not seen or held her precious baby yet. I could only imagine the pain she must have felt after giving birth to a beautiful son and not being able to see him, nor touch him, nor hold him. She looked at me and she asked "Keisha, do you remember what you told me about my baby?" I was confused for a moment because I didn't remember. She said, "You told me that my baby would be born without any problems." Those words ripped into me and touched the depths of my soul. Not only was the devil trying to literally steal her joy, but he was trying to use my presence and God's word to do it! After she reminded me, I remembered praying with her and making that declaration over her when the complications began early in the pregnancy. But I knew that the devil is a liar! All I could do in that moment was to comfort her and to pray to God to show Himself mighty and strong in that hospital for His name's sake. With all of the love, compassion and boldness I could find, I told her to hold steadfast to the promises of God and that He can do anything except fail. That seemed to bring her some comfort. She told us that the doctors told her that her beautiful son was having challenges with his lungs and that there were some other issues that the doctors were concerned about. Once I had the specifics of the situation, I immediately got us together to start praying. We prayed and cried out for the power of God to fall right there in the hospital room. As we continued to pray, we felt the presence of God move through that place and shift the atmosphere. The anointing was flowing freely. We had tapped into and activated God's power to heal, and pleaded the blood of Jesus over her baby. I am telling you there was a move of God in that room, as His Glory filled that place! It felt like God had lifted the roof of the hospital and poured in fresh oil until it overflowed with His Glory. The Glory of the Lord prevailed in a mighty way!

"Comfort, yes, comfort My people! Says your God. Speak comfort to
Jerusalem, and cry out to her, that her warfare is ended, that her
iniquity is pardoned; for she has received from the LORD's hand
Double for all her sins. The voice of one crying in the wilderness:
Prepare the way of the LORD; Make straight in the desert a highway
for our God. Every valley shall be exalted and every mountain and
hill brought low; the crooked places shall be made straight and the
rough places smooth; the glory of the LORD shall be revealed,
and all flesh shall see it together;
for the mouth of the LORD has spoken."
Isaiah 40:1-5

As we continued to pray, the mother of the child was suddenly out of her bed and travailing! I had never heard wailing like that before. She cried out to God to save her baby in a way that only a mother can. It was strong, it was loud, and it was powerful! We began to declare and

decree the word of God over her child's life. I knew that God was going to hear our cry and our prayer because we were praying in His will. In fact, most of our congregation was at the church praying, too. We were at war! I am telling you, I know that God can do anything except fail! Not only did we have the faith to push through to breakthrough, but we had hearts of expectation. We knew beyond a shadow of a doubt that God was going to heal, set free, deliver and restore. We knew that it was already done.

Then he said, "Don't be afraid, Daniel. Since the first day you began to pray for understanding and to humble yourself before your God, your request has been heard in heaven. I have come in answer to your prayer. But for twenty-one days the spirit prince of the kingdom of Persia blocked my way. Then Michael, one of the archangels, came to help me, and I left him there with the spirit prince of the kingdom of Persia.
Daniel 10:12-13 (NLT)

Two days later, I received a text from my friend stating that the hospital planned to release her without the baby. She asked if I would come there and pray for her baby again. I let her know that I would be there and carried on with the rest of my day, continually praying within myself for her and for her baby. That night I hardly slept. I knew breakthrough was in effect and that God was going to do something for her and her baby in that NICU the next day. At around midnight, after much tossing and turning, I called one of my best friends, Susan, and talked to her about the situation with the baby. Susan and I began to pray and cry out for the baby's life and healing and, again, we could feel a fresh anointing, even through the phone. We prayed earnestly and fervently that God would show Himself strong and mighty for this baby and his mother. Susan commanded that the spirit of premature death leave the hospital. Then Susan began to encourage and strengthen me. She reminded me of the story of Elisha and the Shunammite woman. Hallelujah! God is an awesome God! I *needed* to hear this story because I was the vessel that God used to assure my friend that her baby would be healthy and that he would live and not die. Yet, I could not forget my friend's words to me, and the anguish in her voice when she reminded me that I told her that her baby would be healthy. I did tell her that because God had told it to me, now the devil had come along with his lies, trying to get us to believe the wrong reports. I believed God for a miracle. I felt like a modern day Elisha. I read the story again and again until I felt strengthened in the Lord. Now, instead of going to the hospital to pray for my friend's baby's recovery, I was going to that hospital the next day with my natural and God's super and we were going to see a supernatural miracle!

Now it happened one day that Elisha went to Shunem, where there was a notable woman, and she persuaded him to eat some food. So it was, as often as he passed by, he would turn in there to eat some food. And she said to her husband, "Look now, I know that this is a holy man of God, who passes by us regularly. Please, let us make a small upper room on the wall; and let us put a bed for him there, and a table and a chair and a lampstand; so it will be, whenever he comes to us, he can turn in there.
And it happened one day that he came there, and he turned in to the upper room and lay down there. Then he said to Gehazi his servant, "Call this Shunammite woman." When he had called her, she stood before him.
And he said to him, "Say now to her, 'Look, you have been concerned for us with all this care. What can I do for you? Do you want me to speak on your behalf to the king or to the commander of the army?'" She answered, "I dwell among my own people."
So he said, "What then is to be done for her?" And Gehazi answered, "Actually, she has no son, and her husband is old."
So he said, "Call her." When he had called her, she stood in the doorway.
Then he said, "About this time next year you shall embrace a son." And she said, "No, my lord. Man of God, do not lie to your maidservant!"
But the woman conceived, and bore a son when the appointed time had come, of which Elisha had told her.
And the child grew. Now it happened one day that he went out to his father, to the reapers.
And he said to his father, "My head, my head!" So he said to a servant, "Carry him to his mother." When he had taken him and brought him to his mother, he sat on her knees till noon,

and then died.

*And she went up and laid him on the bed of the man of God, shut
the door upon him, and went out. Then she called to her husband,
and said, "Please send me one of the young men and one of the
donkeys that I may run to the man of God and come back."*

*So he said, "Why are you going to him today? It is neither the New
Moon nor the Sabbath." And she said, "It is well."*

*Then she saddled a donkey, and said to her servant, "Drive, and go
forward; do not slacken the pace for me unless I tell you."*

*And so she departed, and went to the man of God at Mount
Carmel. So it was, when the man of God saw her afar off, that he
said to his servant Gehazi, "Look, the Shunammite woman!
Please run now to meet her, and say to her, 'Is it well with you? Is
it well with your husband? Is it well with the child?'"*

And she answered, "It is well."

*Now when she came to the man of God at the hill, she caught him
by the feet, but Gehazi came near to push her away. But the man of
God said, "Let her alone; for her soul is in deep distress, and the
LORD has hidden it from me, and has not told me."*

*So she said, "Did I ask a son of my lord?
Did I not say, 'Do not deceive me'?"*

*Then he said to Gehazi, "Get yourself ready, and take my staff in
your hand, and be on your way. If you meet anyone, do not greet
him; and if anyone greets you, do not answer him;
but lay my staff on the face of the child."*

*And the mother of the child said, "As the LORD lives, and as your
soul lives, I will not leave you." So he arose and followed her.
Now Gehazi went on ahead of them, and laid the staff on the face of
the child; but there was neither voice nor hearing. Therefore he went
back to meet him, and told him, saying,
"The child has not awakened."*

*When Elisha came into the house, there was the child,
lying dead on his bed.*

*He went in therefore, shut the door behind the two of them,
and prayed to the LORD.*

*And he went up and lay on the child, and put his mouth on his
mouth, his eyes on his eyes, and his hands on his hands; and he
stretched himself out on the child,*

and the flesh of the child became warm.
He returned and walked back and forth in the house, and again
went up and stretched himself out on him; then the child sneezed
seven times, and the child opened his eyes.
And he called Gehazi and said, "Call this Shunammite woman."
So he called her. And when she came in to him, he said,
"Pick up your son."
So she went in, fell at his feet, and bowed to the ground;
then she picked up her son and went out."
2 Kings 4:8-37

The next morning, my heart was full and I was overwhelmed with joy as I got dressed to head to the hospital. I knew in my soul that it was well. I anointed my hands with oil and prayed the whole morning. I drove to the hospital continuing to pray with the spirit of expectation. I walked in the room to see my friend up and about with the sound of praise in her voice. She had already been discharged and her aunt was helping her pack up her belongings. I was still overwhelmed by what was in my spirit, but I waited patiently for them to finish. I knew that God was going to do something miraculous, I just didn't know how He would do it! "Keisha, we can go see the baby now," my friend said. I almost fell out because up to now, I didn't expect that we would be able to go into the NICU to see or touch the baby. All I could say was "Thank You, Jesus!"

We walked down the hallway into another area of the maternity ward where we had to scrub down and then were buzzed into the room. I felt like I was walking on holy ground. God was already here. We walked into the room and there he was, just lying there. This tiny little body with tubes connected to almost every part of him. This is the precious little baby that everyone had been praying for. I was finally there, in the room with him getting ready to do what God has called me to do. We walked over to where he was laying and just looked at him for a moment. He had tubes in his nose, an IV in his tiny little hand, a tube in his mouth and something taped to his ankles. We began to pray and to gently touch him from the crown of his head to the soles of his feet. We grew bolder as we spoke the Word of God over his life while touching every part of his body. We commanded his liver, kidneys,

lungs, organs, cells, muscles, heart, bones and every fiber in his body to come under the authority of the blood of Jesus. We prayed for the doctors, the nurses, the other babies that were in there and their families, too. That is the beauty of God's miracles... they are contagious and bless everyone who is around!

Our little baby responded to each of our touches and every word that we declared over his body. We could feel the presence of God permeating the atmosphere in the hospital room. The anointing of God rested, ruled and abode in that place. We knew that we were only the point of contact that God used to bring healing. Our baby was responding to the Word of God and to the presence of God.

But he answered and said, It is written, Man shall not live by bread alone, but by every word that proceedeth out of the mouth of God.
Matthew 4:4

About an hour after I got home from the hospital, I received another text from his mother saying that they are taking him off the tubes and machines. I shouted right there in my kitchen just praising God and thanking Him for breakthrough and victory! Later that evening, I received another text message from her letting me know that they were moving him from the incubator to a regular crib! Again, I released another shout of praise unto our Almighty God! God was moving fast and I was in complete awe and gratitude. God turned a negative report around in less than 24 hours. He did it IMMEDIATELY! The next morning, the mother called me to tell me that her baby was coming home on Tuesday. You have to understand that on Saturday, before we went into the NICU with our precious baby that his doctors said that he would be in the hospital for no less than 2 weeks, maybe even longer because he had a hole in his lungs and some other physical challenges. Now, only 2 days later, his doctors have changed their reports and this baby will be going home in what really comes down to a matter of hours now. God is truly Jehovah Rapha – the God who heals! You have got to _know_ the power that you possess through your position in Christ.

And let us not grow weary while doing good, for in due season we shall reap if we do not lose heart."
Galatians 6:9

We can't lose hope. We are going to reap everything that God has promised in His Word. He is faithful and just. We must know that the Word of God will never fail. We just have to stand on it and never give up. I witnessed a miracle. I always pray that God will show me miracles. God received all the glory and honor. We had a whole team of people praying and believing God with us. To see the Word of God manifested like this was something to behold. The healing power of Jesus! Even if we had 10,000 tongues, we still couldn't praise God enough for showing up and showing out. I am getting teary-eyed now just thinking about it all. God has this baby covered. He is over a year old now and is a strong vessel with no complications.

Be still, and know that I [am] God: I will be exalted among the heathen, I will be exalted in the earth.
Psalm 46:10

Now it is your turn. Do you believe that God can work miracles in your life? Can your faith make you well today? Can your faith grab God's attention? Will you be still enough to feel God's touch today?

I declare to you right now, in this very hour that:

One touch will set you free.
One touch will restore you.
One touch will take you from poverty to prosperity.
One touch will save and deliver you.
One touch will heal you.
One touch will get you out of that mess that you're in.
One touch from the Father and you will never thirst again.
One touch from God and your life will never be the same.

If you would but humble yourself and pray, then God will heal your land. That is a good place to shout if you got the revelation! You won't look back, and you won't go back, because you understand that Jesus

is the true and ultimate fulfiller of your soul, mind and spirit. There is no high that can take you higher than the one that Jesus can give you. Get ready to win in life. Get ready to spring forward. It is time for you to breakthrough, break forth and break loose! It is time to walk in the newness and freshness of God's power, anointing and glory over your life. Allow God to fill those empty pockets in your soul. Go back to the place where you abandoned your faith and cry out for God's grace and glory upon your life. God never left you. You drifted away from Him. Why would God leave His children? No! No! No! We do not serve a deadbeat God. We serve an Almighty God who is Glorious and Righteous in all His ways. Hallelujah!

The effectual fervent prayers of the righteous man availeth much
James 5:16(b)

In other words, the burning, glowing and passionate prayers from your heart and mind will manifest. It's time to start praying with zeal, passion and enthusiasm. It's time to start praying some "Just Because Prayers". "Lord, just because you are God, I praise you!" You must become excited about prayer in your life. Prayer will cause rules and regulations to be revised on your behalf. You must stop playing foolery with God. You must not go to Him in prayer only when all hell breaks loose. You need to pray to keep hell from breaking loose in the first place. You need an honest, open and pure relationship with Jesus. You need to know His desires so that you can pray what's on His heart. He needs to hear your voice in joyful times and in your season of longsuffering.

But the very hairs of your head are numbered.
Matthew 10:30

Even when you are not faithful; God is still faithful. We are a chosen generation and joint heirs with Christ. Jesus loves you. Stop crying and know that you are loved. There is no sin or shame that He won't forgive, no matter what the devil has told you! The devil is a liar, the father of lies and was a liar from the beginning. Christ is your Messiah and He is the True and Living God. He is the giver of life. He loves you in spite of you and your sin. He will provide, for He is Jehovah

Jireh, your provider. He loved you, when you did not even love yourself. Glory! Hallelujah! That is the kind of God you serve. That's why I am so passionate about prayer.

As I look back over the years, I realize that God has delivered me from my fears, my failures and my weakness. He also loved me in spite of myself. It feels like this is the year that I am finally becoming that woman that God created me to be. Now I can clearly see that when I walk by faith, there's nothing that God won't make happen for me. I am making decisions that concern me which line up with my calling in the Kingdom of God. I am seeking His face for answers to my questions. No longer am I asking other people what they think about my life. I am going to God in prayer and believing by faith that He is going to speak to me concerning His plans, visions and the destiny He has for my life.

Now faith is the substance of things hoped for,
the evidence of things not seen.
Hebrews 11:1

Everything about faith requires you to believe, trust, hope and see it in the spirit before God manifests it in the natural. Many times, we only believe God for as long as we can see the promises with our natural eyes, and that's not faith. There are going to be times in your life when all you will have is a vision and a Word from God. However, it's in those times when God really wants you to trust Him and see beyond the natural. The Bible teaches us that manifestation occurs first in the spirit realm. In order to go deeper into the realm of the spirit, you must activate your faith, and if you recall, faith comes by *hearing*. You must open your mouth and declare a thing! It is time for you to take control of your atmosphere.

Assuredly, I say to you, whatever you bind on earth will be bound in
heaven, and whatever you loose on earth will be loosed in heaven.
Matthew 16:19

Open your own mouth and declare that:

> *Faith is limitless and has no boundaries.*
> *Faith is power.*
> *Faith is present.*
> *Faith is future.*
> *Faith is vision.*
> *Faith is now.*
> *Faith requires patience.*
> *Faith is perseverance.*
> *Faith is not giving up or giving in.*
> *Faith is boldness.*
> *Faith is the key to get God's attention.*
> *Faith moves the heart of God and the hand of God.*
> *Faith is long suffering.*

But without Faith it is impossible to please Him, for he who comes must believe that He is, and that He is a rewarder of those who diligently seek Him.
Hebrews 11:6

I have another story to share with you about one of the most tested times in my life. I really had to walk out my faith. However, I am pressed to share it with you to prove to you that God is faithful.

One day while cleaning my room, I laid back to take a break from the cleaning. While rubbing under my arms, I felt a lump in my left breast. So instantly, I began to do self-examination on my breast and indeed it was a lump. I immediately called my mom to tell her what I had found. She assured me that people find irregular lumps all the time in their breast and it was probably nothing. I replied to myself yes that's true but the bottom line is I need to see a doctor to make sure nothing was wrong with my breast.

The next morning I went to see my primary care doctor. My doctor at the time was an amazing physician. Before he could say anything to me, I started to tell him about the lump I found in my breast. I lay on the cold table as he began doing the same exact breast examination I did at home. He confirmed that there was a mass there and scheduled an appointment for me to see a specialist right away.

The following day my mom and I went to see the specialist. There were about 20 women in the waiting room all waiting to see the doctor. I thought to myself someone is not going to receive good news today and I sure hope it's not me. I began to pray to God that He bring me out of this mess. I had been attacked one time too many in my physical body and was tired of fighting. Finally, the nurse called my name and showed me to the examination room. The room was dimly lit and freezing cold! She directed me to remove my blouse and bra and gave me a robe to wear. As I sat there waiting for the doctor to come in, I remember feeling numb. I am only 21 years old and had been going through some really dry and dark places in my life already. By this time the doctor walked in and advised that I would be getting a breast ultra sound. I showed him where I felt the lump and he proceeded with the examination. The next thing I really remember is some very cold gel being placed on my left breast, and then I heard him say, "Now this is interesting". Now, if you are like me, then the last thing you want to hear from a doctor during an exam is the sound of surprise in his voice! He called another doctor into the room and both doctors were taking x-ray on one breast. By this time I am petrified and bawling my eyes out because no one is saying anything to me about what they see, not to mention their exams really hurt and they irritated both of my breasts!

About an hour later, the doctor called my mother and me into another dark room where he had both x-rays up, one of my right breast and one of the left breast. It was obvious that one breast was clear and the left breast was black. He said I had a mass in my left breast. My mom really broke down crying at this point. He said, "Lakeisha; you are going to have a procedure done that will help us to determine if this mass is cancerous or non-cancerous." I was in a state of shock. I said to myself, God I know that you would not do this to me! With all of the pain and agony of the Psoriasis that I am still dealing with, now this, too?! I remember telling my mom once we left the doctor office, "Mom, please don't tell anybody". I knew that I needed time to pray

and take in what I just heard and I surely did not want anyone giving me a death sentence because of their lack of faith and unbelief.

The surgery was scheduled for Tuesday, which was 5 days later. I was sad and depressed, but still soldiering on. I had to work the Sunday before the surgery was scheduled. I was in the restroom at a popular restaurant where I worked preparing for my shift when I started to feel slightly out of it again. I was on the verge of a pity party. I was washing my hands when I heard a small voice say, "You look depressed". "I am", I answered. At this point, I really didn't care who knew that I was depressed because I could no longer hide my pain. The woman didn't say anything else to me for a moment as she continued washing her hands.   When she shut off that water, though, let me tell you something! This lady walked over to me with a holy boldness and touched my breast! She said "You act as though you don't know the God that you serve!" I was caught off guard and for a moment, I was afraid. I had no idea who this lady was and I had not shared any details about me or my situation with her, yet here she was, in my face, reminding me who I am! She then continued to tell me that God healed her from breast cancer and that if I wanted it, if I claimed my healing, that He would heal me, too. All I could manage to say to her was, "I don't even know you", and then I began to cry. She told me to go home, anoint my breast with oil, and walk round my house with Isaiah 53:5 on my breast. This woman never told me her name and I did not ask. That was the last thing on my mind. I was backed up against a wall with this stranger touching me. After she said what she had to say to me, she took her hand off of my breast, turned, and walked out the door. If I had had any doubts about God up to this point, this encounter showed me that He is real in my life. I knew then, beyond the shadow of a doubt that He was bigger and more present than I could ever have imagined.

But He was wounded for our transgressions, He was bruised for our iniquities; the chastisement for our peace was upon Him, and by His stripes we are healed.
Isaiah 53:5

After I got myself together, I left the bathroom and told my boss that I wasn't feeling well and needed to go home. Once I got home I grabbed my oil and anointed my breast. Understand that the power is not in the oil, it is just a point of contact; an act of faith that activates the anointing. I knew that God had already placed healing in my hands and in my body. As an act of obedience, though, I followed her instructions and walked around my house with the Bible literally opened to Isaiah 53:5, and carried the Word of God on my left breast. I prayed and prayed and prayed because I did not want to have that surgery and I knew that God would do something supernatural. You may say, "Lakeisha you did not have to walk with the Bible on your breast", but that was my level of understanding at that time, and don't you know that we serve a God who will meet you at your level of understanding. That's why I love Him like I do! Hallelujah!

The next day I did the same thing and the by time I went to sleep on Monday night, I was still praying to God, and believing Him for a miracle that would keep me from having to have surgery. I was not prepared for what was about to happen next. Sometime in the midnight hour while I was still asleep, something supernatural happened to me. When I woke up on Tuesday morning, the day of the surgery, I had a hole in my breast that was the size of a coin dollar! I started screaming because I could see straight through my breast. I am talking about raw flesh! I ran into my mother's room to show her and she started screaming, too, and asking me what I had done to myself. I told her that I had not done anything and that I had no earthly explanation for what we were seeing. We got dressed and rushed to the specialist to show them what was happening and everyone was shocked. They even started to suggest and insist that I had mutilated my own body. I was offended! Who cuts a hole in their own breast, particularly if they don't want to have surgery?! The team of doctors immediately did another ultra sound, and miraculously, both breasts were clear! There was no evidence of any mass to be found anywhere in my breasts! The doctors were speechless. All they could say was that they still needed to sew up the wound because if they didn't that it would leave a scar. I told them that nobody was touching my breast and that I didn't mind at all living with a scar, which I still have to this day. I know that there are many people who do not believe that God will suspend natural law and perform a miracle that you can see with your own eyes in this day

and age, however, I am grateful to God that He made my mother, Glenda Scavella, and my friend, Susan Cambridge, witnesses to this miraculous, life changing event in my life.

And God confirmed the message by giving signs and wonders and various miracles and gifts of the Holy Spirit whenever he chose.
Hebrews 2:4 (NLT)

Listen, I know that you are probably shocked or incredulous about the story that I just shared with you, but this is my story and every word is true. God did this thing for my good, but for His Glory! I am reminded daily about the amazing God that I serve when I undress myself. My scar is a constant reminder of God's grace and mercy over my life. I am favored and the glory of God is upon me. He sent me my own personal surgeon to remove something that didn't belong to me in the first place. Whose reports will you believe? It takes a personal and intimate relationship with God to experience that kind of supernatural blessing and that is good news. The better news, though, is that God will do the same thing for you! That's why this chapter was so special to me. His glory is what keeps me moving forward. That is why despite all of the negative things that I have been through in my life, I cannot afford to stay in the past, and neither can you. I turned a tombstone into a stepping stone and nobody but God received the glory. This same miraculous power is available to you, too, through obedience and prayer. This is why prayer is so important to me. You get to remind God of his own sovereign Word! For example, Isaiah 53:5 said that I was already healed, so I simply reminded God of His promise and declare it over my own body when I prayed, "God, You said that by your stripes I am healed". You must go to a higher place in *Him*. It's time to trust and depend on God with all of your heart and your mind. You have to believe that He's got your back.

Trust in the LORD with all your heart, and lean not on your own understanding; in all your ways acknowledge Him, and He shall direct your paths.
Proverbs 3:5-6

Hallelujah! I just had to shout again because I remember this testimony so clearly. Faith requires you to go beyond your reasoning and your natural mind and carries you into a place of the supernatural. When you have faith, you are telling God that you trust Him and are so confident that His Word will surely come to pass. You have to believe God's word.

He replied, "Because you have so little faith. I tell you the truth, if you have faith as small as a mustard seed, you can say to this mountain, 'Move from here to there' and it will move. Nothing will be impossible for you.
Matthew 17:20

God is saying all you need is a little faith and He can work with you; and like anything else, the more you use it, the better you become at using it. Your faith will increase! All you have to do is speak and the words that you release from your mouth will go forth and do what you declare. Impossible means not possible to endure. But Jesus teaches that nothing will be impossible for you. My God, that is powerful! Knowledge is power. You will be able to weather the storms of life. It has already been commanded and all you have to do is believe it, declare it and walk in it.

Your faith is a weapon. You *must* have faith. It is not an option, nor up for negotiation. You won't stand a chance without it because your prayers will be ineffectual. Never allow the devil to make you feel as if you don't have any power or authority. You are a child of the Almighty God and are imbued with His power through the shed blood of Jesus Christ. God wants to reward, honor and celebrate you for seeking Him.

But without faith it is impossible to please Him, for he who comes to God must believe that He is, and that He is a rewarder of those who diligently seek Him.
Hebrews 11:6

Let's take another praise break right here!

Celebrate Jesus today for His loving kindness and His tender mercies!!
Celebrate Faith today!
Celebrate Victory today!
Celebrate Joy today!
Celebrate Peace today!
Celebrate Restoration today!
Celebrate Love today!
Celebrate you today!

Father, I thank you for doing a new thing in me right now! I thank you for loving me right now! I thank you for forgiving me my sins right now! I thank you for setting me free and pulling me out of darkness into the light right now! Hallelujah!

For he says, in the time of my favor I heard you, and in the day of salvation I helped you. Now is the time of God's favor, now is the day of salvation.
2 Corinthians 6:2

<u>*Now*</u> is the time for salvation. <u>*Now*</u> is the time for favor. <u>*Now*</u> is the time for grace. <u>*Now*</u> is the time to surrender all you have to your Heavenly Father! I hear the Spirit of the Lord speaking to all those who are reading my book saying:

"Be strong in the Lord and know that I am God. I am The God that sits high and looks low. I am The God that made you more than a conqueror. I am restoring your soul now. I am destroying yolks of bondage and removing the heavy burden now. Stop allowing the devil to hold you back. He has no power in your life unless you give it to him. I have chosen you and the anointing will equip you. I will mend your broken heart and I will renew a right spirit within you. I desire for you to have a consistent prayer life and to keepMe first in your life."

The time is <u>***now***</u> to worship! Finding your place of worship can be an awesome experience. Worship is not necessarily laying prostrate on the floor, or having your head bowed with hands folded together in your face. It's so much more than just that. Your place of worship begins in your heart. Worship is an attitude. It is that tender spot where God touches you. It is where the conviction of His love is so strong that it causes you to seek Him out on increasingly deepening levels, knowing that you are protected and secure. When you worship, the atmosphere changes and the limitless anointing of God overtakes you. Your needs and your desires become those of the Father.

God is Spirit, and those who worship Him must
worship in spirit and truth.
John 4:24

Do you know what a Mountain Goat is? A mountain goat is a species of goat that lives high in the mountains in some parts of the world. Because of the terrain, mountain goats have developed very strong legs and have almost perfect balance. They are able to safely climb rock faces that are much steeper than any that a human or predator can safely climb. They are often referred to as sure-footed, which means that they are not likely to stumble, slip or fall. They are able to climb to the highest part of a mountain without slipping or falling no matter the incline. God has placed this same type of "sure-footedness" in you, which allows you to walk above your situations and circumstances. You are sure footed in Jesus Christ! He won't allow you to fall!

He will not allow your foot to be moved;
He who keeps you will not slumber. Behold,
He who keeps Israel shall neither slumber nor sleep
Psalm 121:3-4

Prepare your heart and mind for worship. Tell the Lord how much you love Him, make it personal. Let Him know how much you adore Him. Thank Him for waking you up this morning and starting you on your way. This is between you and God. "Hallelujah!" is the highest praise, so give it to Him now! Wow! I can sense a sweet spirit in the atmosphere because God is pulling you through right now. Keep worshipping Him in your own way, thanking Him for all He has done and will do in your life. Where would you be were it not for God on your side? You may not be where you want to be, but praise God,

you're not where you used to be! Get ready to walk in victory. Be all that God created you to be. Be fulfilled in knowing that you have a Comforter. God loves you and so do I.

You are an Individual of Prayer!

Practice praying. Use the space below to write a letter to God. It can be about anything you need it to be. Address Him in whatever manner you feel most comfortable with. Some people call Him "Daddy", some call Him "Father", some call Him "God". You call Him whatever you believe your relationship with Him is, or what you want it to be. Remember, prayer is a personal conversation with Him, so write what you have to say, and listen for what He says back. If you are seeking answers, then write His responses, too. Once your letter is complete, then read it out loud. That is your prayer!

_____

_____

_____

_____

_____

_____

_____

_____

_____

_____

_____

_____

_____

_____

_____

_____

_____

LAKEISHA DIXON

Chapter 5

Power
"The Authority"

This is the "Sizzle" chapter! Power produces energy and energy produces action! Get excited and let's get moving!

Power! Power! Power! Power! Do you have it? Do you want it? Do you speak it? There is power in the name of Jesus! There is power in the Blood of Jesus! There is power to remove burdens and destroy yokes! There is power to heal the sick! There is power to cast out devils! There is power to get wealth! There is power in the words that you speak! In this chapter, I am going to teach you how to speak with authority and power! You are going to produce a life of greatness with the words that you speak! You are going to begin to speak words of life and not death; blessings and not curses; prosperity and not poverty; and words of victory and not defeat!

Power is the ability to do or act; it is strength, might, force, or authority; it is the possession of control; it is energy or momentum; it is to inspire and sustain; it is influence; and it is ability. Where is your power? The time is now to resurrect every dead thing in your life with the power of your words. Can you remember any of the dead and lifeless words that you have spoken into your life? Things said in a moment of anger, sadness or in a state of rage? Perhaps, you may have

spoken words of death after a doctor's report. What has been the result of something negative you have spoken into existence? It is time for you to take control of your life and win! It begins with you eliminating negative words of hopelessness, despair and defeat! For example, "I will never", "I am broke", "I am poor", "I can't", "I'm at a dead end", "if it ain't one thing it's another", "I'm a failure". All of these confessions, and any other negative declarations like them, HAVE GOT TO GO! They must be replaced with words like, "I can", "I will", "I win", "I've got the victory", "I am an overcomer", "I am destined for greatness", "It shall come to pass", "I have power to triumph over the devil", "this battle is not mine but the Lord's", "I am a royal priesthood", "I am a chosen generation", "I was born to win and reign in victory". My God! My spirit is fired up because I just declared the true and living Word of God! The more I speak the Word of God, the more I believe His promises.

The tongue has the power of life and death,
and those who love it will eat its fruit.
Proverbs 18:21

Living life with limits and borders just won't do. God has called you out and launched you forward to be abundantly blessed. However, it is going to be based on what you speak and think. It is time for you to get your mind right and open your mouth and say something great! It's time for you to recognize just how powerful you are. My God! Get rid of that old way of thinking. Just because someone told you what they think or how they feel doesn't mean that it's true. Remember, what other people think about you is none of your business! Get out the box and speak with power and authority.

Now to Him who is able to do exceedingly abundantly above all that
we ask or think, according to the power that works in us
Ephesians 3:20

When I think about power, I think about a driving force, a push behind a person or thing. I think about God placing His super on our natural and making us supernatural beings. For example, the light from a flashlight makes life easier when there's darkness all around, however, if there is no power source, such as the batteries which power the flash light, it cannot be used for what it was created for. Once the power source for the flashlight is restored, then the flashlight can be used for the purpose that it was created for. In the same way, when we are not connected to our power source, we cannot be used for the purpose that we were created for. This, then, begs the question, who or what is your power source? For me, the answer is Christ, so this lets me know that without Christ in my life that my life is void, ineffective and empty. I will grope in darkness. Without Christ I would have no power, no ability, no energy and no control. Without Christ I would be lost and on a path of destruction and death.

But you shall receive power when the Holy Spirit has come upon you.
Acts 1:8

Who is the Holy Spirit? He is our Truth, our Advocate, our Comforter, and He leads and guides us in the right direction. Jesus promised us that when He ascended to be with the Father that He would send us a Helper.

Nevertheless, I tell you the truth. It is to your advantage that I go away; for if I do not go away, the Helper will not come to you; but if I depart, I will send Him to you. And when He has come, He will convict the world of sin and of righteousness and of judgment: of sin
John 16:7-9

We just read here that the Holy Spirit will bring conviction, not condemnation. I remember once becoming very upset with someone and speaking to that person in a way that was not pleasing or acceptable in the sight of God. Afterwards, I felt so bad. I felt a nudge from the Holy Spirit saying "You were wrong. Go back, apologize and make it right." Has that ever happened to you? If so, then that was godly conviction from the Holy Spirit.

Therefore, there is now no condemnation
for those who are in Christ Jesus.
Romans 8:1

There is a major difference between conviction and condemnation. Condemnation is negative and degrading. It offers no redemption and is designed only to punish. It is relentless and will stalk you forever if you allow it to. Conviction, however, is positive. It is restorative and redemptive. It offers the opportunity to correct mistakes and bring healing in the place of offense. Hallelujah! Thank you Jesus! There is no condemnation because we are in Christ Jesus, your Redeemer. Keep in mind this scripture is for those who believe. Mark 16:16 teaches us that those who do not believe will be condemned, but thank God, again, that He has commissioned me and you to go out to the hedges and highways to declare the good news of the gospel! As a believer, I have got to give God praise for that because the world will stone you to death for any mistakes that you make. However, God is saying, I am not going to condemn you, I am going to cover you. Don't allow the devil to attack your mind because you made a few mistakes. You are covered by the blood of the Lamb. Now, by no means am I telling you that sin doesn't bring consequences; rather, what I am telling you is that God is faithful and just to forgive you of your sins. When you have a relationship with Christ you receive access to the Holy Spirit. Read some of the benefits you will inherit just by receiving Christ. Keep in mind, though, that everything is activated by your words.

"So too the [Holy] Spirit comes to our aid and bears us up in our weakness; for we do not know what prayer to offer nor how to offer it worthily as we ought, but the Spirit Himself goes to meet our supplication and pleads in our behalf with unspeakable yearnings and groanings too deep for utterance."
Romans 8:26 (AMP)

"He makes intercession for the saints according to the will of God."
Romans 8:27 (NKJ)

Do you know how powerful those scriptures are? That means even at your weakest point, or deepest valley, even when you can't or don't feel like praying, even when the pain is unbearable and you cannot speak – God's Holy Spirit is praying for you. My God! You ought to give God some praise for that! Not only will He pray for you but He only prays according to the will of the Father. Hallelujah! This is why

70

it is so important sometimes when you are going through to watch what you say. There's no need to speak words of defeat when the Holy Spirit is standing in the gap praying for you. You have benefits because of your relationship with God. You are never alone. You have power because the Holy Spirit will teach you all things and He will comfort you. You have to know as a believer that you have access to everything that God has ordained for you. God will reveal His mysteries to you through His Holy Spirit. You will receive revelations about things that you previously couldn't even conceive of. Revelation is making known something that was previously concealed. God will withhold revelation until such time that you are spiritually mature in some areas and your natural mind can grasp what He has to show you. The more you study His Word, the more revelation you will receive; and once you are ready and able to receive, He will show you in His Word.

Now, having been filled with the Holy Spirit, I understand that I must be ever mindful of the words I allow to come out of my mouth. Your words have strength, force, drive and influence. Let's take it a step further; your words have usable power, quick energy and expression. Therefore, when words are released out of your mouth they quickly go to work to bring to pass what you have spoken, whether positive or negative. This is why God speaks about His Word being powerful.

Then God said, "Let Us make man in our image, according to our likeness"; So God created man in His own image; in the image of God He created him; male and female He created them.
Genesis 1:26-27

For the word of God is living and powerful, and sharper than any two edge sword, piercing even to the marrow, and is discerner of the thoughts and intents of the heart.
Hebrews 4:12

My God, this is powerful! We are created in the image and in the likeness of God! This is not news, but it should be revelatory! Since God made you both in His image and in His likeness, that means you look like him and you can do what he can do. When parents have children, those children generally look like their parents and can do

71

what their parents can do, right? If the parents have two eyes, then the child has two eyes. If the parents can walk and speak, even though the child has not learned to walk and speak yet, he or she was born with the ability, and the necessary body parts to be able to eventually learn to walk and speak. Likewise, since His Words are living, powerful and sharp, then that means that your words are living, powerful and sharp! What have you caused to live or die in your life with the words you have spoken? As children, we were taught that "words could never hurt". It turns out that's just not true. Words have weight and substance. You can tear a person down with words, or build them up. Words, not only have the ability to hurt, but words have the ability to kill. They can kill a soul, a mind or a spirit. The wrong words can abort dreams and visions and can paralyze faith.

Is not my word like a fire? Says the Lord, and like a hammer that breaks the rock in pieces.
Jeremiah 23:29

Hallelujah! These are powerful images! Fire and Hammers can be used to destroy and to create, to purify, to shape and to mold. That verse simply means that you can do whatever you say you can do; you can have whatever you say you can have; and you can be whatever you say you can be. God has already given you the tools to shape your life into whatever you want it to be. So no matter what the devil tries to throw at you, you can use your mouth like a hammer to destroy the works of the devil. Don't get tricked into believing the wrong things because then you might say the wrong things. Destroy negative thoughts with the Word of God.

Did you know that a word will cancel a thought every time? Try this exercise: In your mind, count to 100 in multiples of 10, i.e., 10, 20, 30, etc. At the same time, say your home address out loud. What happened? Were you able to keep counting in your mind while you were speaking? Or did you have to stop counting, speak your address, and then pick up where you left off in your count? Do you see how this works?

There is a very strong connection between your mouth, your ears and your brain, but your mouth can cause your brain to change the way that it sees, hears, thinks and believes. So, when doubt, fear, unbelief, lack, sickness and disease come your way, use your hammer to destroy it. It is time for you to begin to open up your mouth to declare and decree something great. Don't give the devil anymore glory. Your mouth is your weapon. You have <u>power</u> to triumph over the devil and your enemies. You have power to bind every stronghold in your family, in your mind, on your job, in your finances and in your ministry. You have been given the power to do so. Walk in your kingdom authority as a child of God with dunamis, Holy Ghost power! Thank you Jesus! The Word of God is alive today. God created the earth with the words that He spoke. For every problem that He ever wanted to solve He spoke the solution into existence. From the very beginning He used words to carry out actions and achieve results.

In the beginning was the Word, and the Word was with God,
and the Word was God.
John 1:1

I have another story to tell you. You must be thinking that I am a human pin cushion by now! Praise God that I have joy unspeakable. I have received beauty for my ashes. There was a time when I needed to have a liver biopsy. My doctor requested the procedure due to the potency of the medication that I was taking for the Psoriasis. While I was being prepped for the procedure I asked my nurse several times when she was going to administer the local anesthesia. She finally told me that the doctor who was performing the procedure would be in shortly and would answer any questions that I had. This made me very nervous. My mother was there, as usual, for moral and mental support. The exam room was very cold and the lights were extra bright.

The doctor finally came into the room to perform what I thought was going to be a minor procedure. He came over to me and before I knew it I was in excruciating pain! This procedure was being performed on me with NO ANESTHESIA! I was horrified and in unbelievable pain! He continued with the procedure and took a sample of my liver, completely oblivious to my screams of pain! I was wide awake and I felt everything, even after being assured that I would only feel a bit of

pressure during the procedure, but no pain. Finally, he removed the object that he used to excise that small portion of my liver and I felt a small bit of relief, but it was only short lived because he told me that he was going to have to take a second piece. I was devastated. I had never experienced pain like that before in my life, and up to now it seemed like my life was go to work, go to church, go to the doctor, be in pain! My mother did all that she could to try to help me to get through it, but nothing was helping. Finally, she told me to just call on the name of Jesus, but I was in so much pain, I could not even speak. I cried so hard and so much. About 2 hours after this nightmare of a procedure was over, while I was in the recovery room, an older lady who I didn't know came into the room, closed the door and told me to get out the bed and began to praise God now for a healthy liver. My mom told the lady that I couldn't move because she's in too much pain. The woman told my mother boldly that I was to get out of that bed and praise God! My mom knew that when it came to my faith and being obedient to the word that I would do what I was told to do. I managed to stand up, lifted my hands up to heaven and began to bless the name of the Lord. I had no idea who this nurse was. She told me it is going to take up to 1week for my test results to come back. However, I needed to start praising God now like I already have the victory. My God! Needless to say, the doctor's report came back and my liver was healthy. I know God to be a healer and a doctor in a sick room. Hallelujah!

God has always sent me a WORD through someone about my health and healing. I truly believe because of the praises that went up in advance that God opened the windows of heaven and touched my body. That's why when it comes to healing and restoration no one can tell me what God can't do. I only know and understand what God WILL DO. I have seen so many miracles in my life concerning my health. I have trusted that God would bring me through and He has been faithful. I know that His Word is a healing balm for my soul, mind and internal organs. Pastor Regina Lamb use to always say "You confess the Word until you see a manifestation, never stop confessing the Word of God." God will always show Himself strong. The question is can you handle the process?

*But he answered and said, It is written, Man shall not live by bread
alone; but man lives by every word that proceeds
from the mouth of the Lord.*
Matthew 4:4

You can't survive in this world with your own bread of knowledge and
understanding for food and sustenance. You need the knowledge and
power of God. You need Fresh Manna from Heaven daily. Everything
about the Word of God is life, truth, revelation and power. You have
got to get a revelation about this power that's in the Word of God. The
time is now to beat up and beat back the devil with your words. God
has touched your mouth.

*Then the Lord put forth His hands and touched my mouth, and the
Lord said to me: behold, I have put My words in your mouth. See, I
have this day set you over the nations and over the kingdoms, to root
out and to pull down, to destroy and to throw down,
to build and to plant"*
Jeremiah 1:9

Hallelujah! Isn't it something to behold when God touches your
mouth? His touch is so powerful that it will burn everything that
doesn't sound like Him out of your mouth. Your conversation will
change, your tone will change, and your words will begin to line up
according to the will and purpose of God for your life. When God
touches your mouth, you have no choice but to speak life.
Furthermore, when God touches your mouth you will be able to root
up, pull out and utterly destroy some previous things you may have
planted in times of despair and hopelessness. Glory be to the most
High God! His touch will destroy the works of the devil from your life
and throw down every giant of defeat and negative word that was ever
spoken over you. When God touches your mouth you can build and
bring to pass your visions, dreams and destiny. You can plant seeds
into your loved ones for salvation, deliverance and restoration.
Hallelujah! The power of God is available to you right now! You ought
to give God praise for that right now! Glory! Hallelujah!

And when He had called His twelve disciples to Him, He gave them power over unclean spirits, to cast them out, and to heal all kinds of sickness and all kinds of disease."
Matthew 10:1

There was another time in my life when I was just overtaken by heaviness and sadness. In the late 80's, my aunt was diagnosed with HIV/AIDS from a husband who was living an undercover life as a gay man. She was pregnant with my little cousin at the time, who was also born with HIV/AIDS. He only lived to be 4 years old. As I entered my sophomore year of high school I found out that I was losing yet another aunt to HIV/AIDS. By the time I was a senior in high school, I was losing yet a third aunt to this horrible disease! I was in a state of confusion, anger, and bitterness. How could this happen to our family? I was devastated because the issue was never confronted. It was just a big family secret. What I have realized is that no devil should ever be able to keep my mouth shut because of an issue that I didn't want to confront. I learned that I had to tackle the enemy with the Word of God. God never hid from or entertained the devils; he cast them out.

I often wonder what would truly happen if we were to tap into the power, ability, energy, force and control that God has given to us. Can you imagine the possibilities of miracles, healing and breakthroughs that you would encounter just from tapping into this kind of power that God has already given you? God has commissioned you to perform His Word. Oftentimes, though, fear causes many to miss opportunities to make a difference in the lives of others.

And from the days of John the Baptist until now the kingdom of heaven suffereth violence, and the violent take it by force.
Matthew 11:12

The stigma associated with the disease, and our limited understanding of how it was transmitted, contributed to my family's silence. It's like we became part of the enemy's conspiracy against ourselves. No one wanted to talk about the fact that all three of my aunts had died from the same disease. The time finally came when I decided that I was not going to sit around and keep quiet about the truth. Who's going to step up and interrupt this spirit of affliction and disease that was causing premature death in my generational line? I cried out from my soul. I decided that the buck stops with me! No more lies! No more excuses! No more! I refused to lose another loved one to this disease. I was set and determined when I prayed out loud "Satan, you are a liar and the father of lies. I can't and I won't continue to sit back and allow this to happen in my family!" I understood that I could never allow the enemy to be the head or our home and then act like I didn't see him. I understood that I had to cut that head off! I heard someone say, that the devil is 100% evil.

Soon after that declaration, my pastor had an altar call for those who had been holding on to something from their past. He told us that if we wanted to be free from it that we were to write it down and bring it to the altar. I wrote, "I will not be a victim of AIDS. I will not die from AIDS."

Because you speak this word,
Behold, I will make My words in your mouth fire.
Jeremiah 5:14

God had placed so much fire in my mouth that I began to boldly confess the Word of God and to really believe that generational curses were being destroyed. I began to devour and destroy all demonic assignments over my life and those to follow. I interrupted the plan of Satan with the Word of God. I knew I had the fire of God in my mouth and I was not going to allow the devil to keep me quiet about a demonic spirit that was running rampant in my family and not cry out for the glory of God to intervene! I knew that the grace of God and the mercy of God were sufficient for my needs. I knew that both of my grandmothers, Sarah and Estell, had passed the mantle of prayer, power and worship on to me. I was determined to run the race that was set before me. I was determined to beat the odds. I was determined not to minimize my value and integrity as a believer to accommodate sin in my life. I was determined to be a vessel that God could and would use. I am free from the bondage of sin because of Christ!

As, I write this, I am in tears because if I had known back then what I

know now, I would have prayed and added more years to my aunt's lives. This is so heavy for me to write but I have got to get it out. I know that this testimony will help someone. I am an intercessor; I stand between God and judgment pleading on the behalf of someone else.

And I sought for a man among them, that should make up the hedge,
and stand in the gap before me for the land,
that I should not destroy it: but I found none.
Ezekiel 22:30

I believe that more of us do not see generational curses destroyed because we won't access the power that is already working in us by opening our mouths and declaring a thing to be or to cease. It seems we have become afraid to confront devils. Whether you believe in them or not, they do exist. If God has truly given you power, why are you afraid? I have seen too many miracles in my own life not to believe or trust God's Word. That's how confident I am about the Word of God. When pressure is applied to the Word of God it will explode into a supernatural miracle. God is a healer, a deliverer and a redeemer.

Watching my aunts die from AIDS impacted my life in a major way. I have managed, with the grace of God, to live a lifestyle of holiness and submission to my Heavenly Father. I now boldly confess, after years of embarrassment and shame that even at the age of 32 years old, I am still a virgin. You don't always know the lessons you will learn from a trial or a test. I made this vow back in high school not realizing, I would still be a virgin at 32. I used to believe that by the age of 25 I would have been married with at least 2 kids. I heard someone say, tell God your plans and He will laugh. Has it been easy walking in the shoes of a virgin? NO! I tell people all the time, I have desires and urges just like any other healthy, functioning human being. Virgins have feelings too! (LOL). I do want companionship, however I realize that unlike diamonds, rubies are hard to find, and I would be a fool to play Russian roulette with my life after watching my aunts die.

Take my advice today. Your body is the temple of the living God. Don't jump on the clearance rack and mark yourself down just to be purchased by another person. Understand that you were already purchased by the Blood of Jesus and that makes you priceless. You are not a dime piece, you are a master piece, created by the Master of Peace! You can never be "for sell". You must be earned, discerned, honored, respected and celebrated. Never give up on the promises of God. Stand still and stand firm on your confessions of faith and expectations.

My people are destroyed for lack of knowledge.
Hosea 4:6

What is knowledge? Knowledge is information and skills acquired through experience or education; facts and information. Without knowledge, you may find yourself in some dangerous situations. Now you may be thinking that I have bound myself to the fear and torment of believing that every potential mate already has HIV/AIDS and is just hell-bent on giving it to me. You would have been right some time ago because there was a time when I was really ignorant on the subject of STD's, including HIV/AIDS. I had to become educated and informed about STD's. I learned to stop saying, "I don't know what that means" and began to inquire and ask questions. I declare to you that everyone needs to know their HIV status. No one should ever say, "I don't know because I've never been tested." This is practical advice for your life right today. People are dying not just from diseases and curses, but from a lack of knowledge. That scripture is not just to be used in the spiritual realm but also in the natural. Don't become ruined or die because you refuse facts and information.

And the LORD shall make thee the head, and not the tail; and thou shalt be above only, and thou shalt not be beneath;
Deuteronomy 28:13(a)(b)

Whose reports will you believe? I am reminded of the story of Moses and the twelve spies. God had promised the Children of Israel that he would lead them into the promised land. A land that flowed with milk and honey known as Cannan. God instructed Moses to choose a man from each tribe to go and spy out the land so that Moses could plan out their attack. The twelve went out and came back some days later

saying that the land was indeed a rich and prosperous land, but that there was a problem. The land was filled with giants and mighty fighting men. Ten of the twelve told Moses that they did not believe that Israel should go to war with these people because they didn't see how they could ever win. In fact, they went on to explain how their own hearts failed them for fear and that even to themselves they were like grasshoppers when compared to the inhabitants of this land. However two of the twelve, Joshua and Caleb, believed not only that they should go to war, but that if they did go to war that they would win the battle because the Lord was on their side! As a result of their boldness, Joshua and Caleb, with their families, were the only people of their generation to actually make it into the Promised Land; while the ten and everyone of their families over the age of twenty years old never made it into the Promised Land. Caleb and Johsua spoke as men of valor, power and relentless faith, and they were richly rewarded for it. Joshua even ended up replacing Moses as the leader of Israel once his time was finished.

If you confess with your mouth the Lord Jesus and believe in your heart that God has raised Him from the dead, you will be saved. For with the heart one believes unto righteousness and with the mouth confession is made unto salvation.
Romans 10:9-10

Can you imagine being chosen to carry out an assignment for the Lord and coming back with a bad report? Of the twelve who were heirs to the promise, who had already seen the miracle of their freedom from Egypt, their deliverance from Pharaoh and manna from heaven, only two were able to attain the promise. All of these men had the same knowledge, but only two seemed to also possess wisdom and understanding. Joshua and Caleb recognized their respective positions in God's Kingdom and stood on the authority that was given to them. The other ten could not see themselves in the way that God saw them. This is a perfect example of clouded faith, lack of faith, useless words, distorted mindset, unbelief and negative thinking. They did not understand their value that was already placed on the inside of them. These men allowed what they saw with their natural eyes to overtake the sight of their spiritual eyes. Their words were powerless, null and void. You can lose a battle before it even begins by thinking and believing the wrong things. When you don't believe in yourself, you'll never bet on yourself. You will bet on other people, the lottery and a sporting game because you esteem those things higher than your own value. However, when it comes to investing the Word of God into your mind and your heart, you allow the devil to sabotage your time with God and as a result you never conceive the things that God speaks about you. I declare to you that you are beautiful and anointed. You are victorious!

> *Do not waste time arguing over godless ideas and old wives' tales.*
> *Instead, train yourself to be godly.*
> ***1Timothy 4:7***

Refuse to be a grasshopper. When words are released out of your mouth it gives the thing you said permission to exist. Words are seeds and when planted they will take root on something, whether it is positive soil or negative soil. It will bring back what you have spoken. Be mindful of the words you speak and become an Individual of Power. Be fulfilled, my friend, knowing that prayer can change everything. God can turn your life around instantly. Below is another exercise that you can use to train yourself to be godly. These are Confessions of Power! Use this list to practice opening up your mouth and saying something great!

Declare these things with power and authority! *I am!*

> *I am Powerful!*
> *I am Possible!*
> *I am wonderfully and fearfully made!*
> *I am a Winner!*
> *Christ died so that I can have Life!*
> *I am Wealthy!*
> *I am Healthy!*
> *I am Motivated!*
> *I am Determined!*
> *I am Free from the bondage of sin!*
> *I am Redeemed!*

Today is a Great Day!
I am predestined for Greatness!
God is on my side!
I choose not to fear!
I am Valuable!
God is giving me witty ideas today!
I have the Word of God inside of me!
I am Beautiful!
All generational curses are destroyed!
I am Healed!
I walk in total victory!
I am an over comer!
I am loaded daily with blessings!
God is making my name great!
I am accepted into the kingdom of God!
God is blessing my business!
I have favor with God and man today!
I celebrate my life today!
I am a new creation in Christ!
I believe in myself when others don't!
I expect great things to happen to me today!
I am mentally alert!
Money knows my name and my voice and it comes to me now!
I know God's voice and the voice of a stranger I shall not follow!
I was created by the Best!
I am an Individual of Prayer!
I am an Individual of Purpose!
I am an Individual of Passion!
I am an Individual of Perseverance!
I am an Individual of Prosperity!
I am an Individual of Power!
I am an Individual of Purging!

By now you may be thinking, "Lakeisha, I want to know how to be a Victorious Individual of Power. I have gone through a lot of trials and tests in my life and I want to be free from the bondage of sin. I need the Helper to be in my life, which is the Holy Spirit, to be my guide, my comforter, my advocate and my intercessor. I need to learn how to speak like a victor and not a victim." I am excited that you want to see change and breakthrough in your life. First, you must repent and invite Him into your heart. Say this prayer with me and confess it out loud. This is personal prayer between you and God.

> *Father, come into my heart. Forgive me of my sins, known and unknown. Wash me in the blood of your precious son Jesus. I apply the blood of Jesus over my mind, body, spirit and soul. Purify my spirit and create in me a clean heart. I believe that because you died on the cross for me I am free, I am redeemed and I am completely forgiven. I believe that you were beaten, died on a cross, were buried and rose again on the third day to save me. Transform my thinking, mend my broken heart and come live on the inside of me. Activate the Holy Spirit within me. I want your power. I need your glory. I desire to live a life that's pleasing in your sight. I know that You will perfect everything that concerns me and my lifestyle. I surrender all to You for You are my King. I give You praise and glory in Jesus Name! Amen.*

If you prayed this prayer the angels in heaven are rejoicing. I declare and decree that your life will never be the same because of your commitment to Christ! You have been redeemed and bought with a price. Hallelujah! You will make mistakes and even fall sometimes but this time the blood is on your side to forgive you, make you clean and wash you clean.

Salvation simply means: deliverance from sin, captivity, death, and liberation from ignorance. Jesus has redeemed you from the hands of the enemy, through the blood that He shed on the cross at Calvary.

The Victorious State of Mind

For God so loved the world that He gave His only begotten son,
that whosoever believes in Him should not perish
but have everlasting life.
John 3:16

So I say to you, ask, and it will be given to you; seek and you will
find, knock, and it will be opened to you.
Luke 11:9

Take some time to reflect on the goodness and mercy of God and write
down some of your feelings and thoughts. Use the space below to
write down your prayer needs and believe that you receive in Jesus
name.

_____

_____

_____

_____

_____

_____

_____

_____

_____

_____

_____

_____

_____

_____

_____

_____

_____

_____

84

LAKEISHA DIXON

Chapter 6

Perseverance
"The Strength"

_Don't you realize that in a race everyone runs, but only one person
gets the prize? So run to win!_
1Corinthians 9:24

So far I have shared with you that you were created for a purpose, that
you have to purge destructive habits and wrong thinking in order to
access your passions, and that by opening your mouth in prayer you
activate your power. Now, I want to talk to you about perseverance.
You have accessed some great practical advice in this book. All praise,
honor and glory to God! However, it will all have been for naught if
you do not persevere until the end. When is the end? What's waiting
for you there? You won't know that until you see God, but there are
some clues in our life that you can draw from. Ask yourself, do you
believe that you are presently doing what God called you to do? If you
are not, then you probably have some more things through which you
must persevere. If you are walking in your purpose, then ask yourself
have you completed all of your assignments. Chances are that you
have not, because one assignment leads to another in the Kingdom, so
it is likely that you, too, have some persevering to do.

Do you have what it takes to stay in the race? Do you have what it

takes to maintain your position of faith even in stressful situations? You have been summoned to hold on and to not give up. You must remember that the journey is not the destination. The journey is the passage from one season of life to another. At times your journey will be long and in this process you will experience growth, pain, healing, restoration, warfare, grace, mercy, salvation, revelation and so much more to create in you relentless faith and persistence. It is during these times when you will really need the Word of God to be a lamp unto our feet.

> *Your word is a lamp to my feet and a light to my path.*
> **Psalm 119:105**

God's Word is going to light the pathway towards your destination. Be steadfast! Be unmovable! Be zealous! God will give you strength to get through your darkest valley. God is always with you according to the Word of God in Psalm 23:4. Your reward is on the way but you must endure. Perseverance relates directly to endurance. It means to be steadfast, to display tenacity and to actively maintain in spite of difficulty. Wow! Just take some time to really think about this for a moment, to be steadfast (stand strong), to have tenacity (hold fast), to endure and maintain in difficult situations, which is probably the hardest part. Everyone doesn't have what it takes to stand and wait on the Lord. In this present age we have become used to the quick and fast way of doing things and don't know how to wait. Likewise, people don't want to wait on the promises of God. Honestly, how many people do you know personally who spend an hour or more in prayer or communion with God? One of the reasons that many people do not see the promises of God come to pass in their lifetime is because they lack what it takes to receive, which is perseverance. Tarrying, or waiting on the Lord, seems to be lost in the Church.

> *But let patience have [her] perfect work,*
> *that ye may be perfect and entire, wanting nothing.*
> **James 1:4**

God is not a magician or a trick horse, sitting around waiting for you to say a few words or snap your fingers so that He has something to do. God is not subject to your flesh; therefore, He is not moved by your emotions. Temper tantrums do not get His attention. He will occasionally allow trials and tribulations in your life in order to get you to a place of reverence, or learning, or gratitude. For this, you should rejoice! If ever there was a time that we all needed endurance to make it through that time would be now.

Therefore do not cast away your confidence, which has great reward.
For you have need of endurance, so that after you have done the will
of God, you may receive the promise
Hebrews 10:35-36

In other words, endurance is the capacity, the backbone, courage, patience and tolerance to stand. After you have done these things you will receive the promise. What is the promise? Everything that God has promised you in His Word. The problem is, we want the promises of God but don't always want to endure. The Word of God is giving us clear directions. Don't cast away your confidence because it has a great reward. Our trials and our tribulations are meant to build something very important in us.

Consider it pure joy, my brothers, whenever you face trials of many
kinds, because you know that the testing of your faith develops
perseverance. Perseverance must finish its work so that you may be
mature and complete, not lacking anything.
James 1:2-4 (NIV)

Hallelujah! The Bible says consider it a clean, spotless and a delightful pleasure when you face trials. When your faith is being tested, it means that God is developing you in an area of your life where you need to grow. He is pushing you forward, building your strength and character, and teaching you to overcome. Now, James also teaches that there is an amount of maturing that takes place while you are persevering. It is not your age, however, which makes you mature; rather, it is your growth as a result of experiences that determine your next level of maturity. Therefore, a person can seem mature in the natural, but may not be spiritually mature and grounded in the Word of God. "Perseverance must finish its work so that you may be mature and

complete, not lacking anything". So, if your faith is not being tested then you should probably ask yourself what side of the fence are you on. Who are you rolling with? Hmmmm... The answer may surprise you!

And if it seem evil unto you to serve the LORD, choose you this day whom ye will serve; whether the gods which your fathers served that [were] on the other side of the flood, or the gods of the Amorites, in whose land ye dwell: but as for me and my house, we will serve the LORD.
Joshua 24:15

God gives us strength to stand in every season of pressing so that we can endure. In some seasons it is easy to hold on. Anybody can stand when all the bills are paid, marriage is all together, there's no sickness and disease, children are good and you have money in the bank. However, how do you stand when everything is being tested and tried at the same time? Can you stand and see the salvation of the Lord? You must learn to not fight, but actively wait on the Lord to deliver you to victory, which is a skill learned only as you continue to persevere.

You will not need to fight in this battle. Position yourselves, stand still and see the salvation of the LORD, who is with you, O Judah and Jerusalem! Do not fear or be dismayed; tomorrow go out against them, for the LORD is with you.
2 Chronicles 20:17 (NLT)

No matter what position you are in, you must understand that He is with you. When you are feeling weary or tired, pray this prayer:

> *Lord, have mercy on me when I am feeling weary and fatigued.*
> *Lord, forgive me for not enjoying the journey for growth opportunities.*
> *Lord, forgive me for wanting the victory without the fight.*
> *Lord, forgive me for wanting the healing without the endurance.*

Lord, forgive me for wanting forgiveness without forgiving.

Lord, forgive me for wanting the baby but aborting the birthing process.

Lord, forgive me for wanting the rainbow without the storm.

Lord, forgive me for wanting the gift and disregarding the packaging.

Lord, forgive me for complaining when I should have been worshipping.

Lord, forgive me for sinning when I should have been praying.

Oh, God show me Your mercy even now as I read. I humble myself before You right now and I choose to serve You in spirit and in truth. Lord, order my steps as I prepare to do Your will and not my own will, Father. Amen.

Therefore, my beloved brethren, be steadfast, immovable, always abounding in the work of the Lord, knowing that your labor is not in vain in the Lord.
1 Corinthians 15:58

You better go ahead and give God some praise right now for His Word! Your labor is not in vain. In other words, your labor will be successful, having great purpose and worth. It is priceless. You cannot even imagine the value that you have as a child of God. You are pregnant with possibility. Some people have been walking around pregnant in the spirit for way too long. Is this you? Baby, if no one ever told you before, it is time for you to give birth in the spirit. God is saying it is time to push. Yes, there will be pain because of the gifting, the talents, the anointing and the power that you possess. There is greatness wrapped up inside of you. What's in you must be birthed in the spirit in order to be made manifest into the natural. I know that you might be afraid but you must go through the process. No one else is going to treat your spiritual baby the way God wants you to treat it. PUSH! Bear down and push out! Stop wasting time and get on the course that is your destiny. You have a divine assignment that God predestined even before the foundations of the world. Hallelujah!!!

Hast not thou made an hedge about him, and about his house, and about all that he hath on every side? thou hast blessed the work of his hands, and his substance is increased in the land. But put forth thine hand now, and touch all that he hath, and he will curse thee to thy face. And the LORD said unto Satan, Behold, all that he hath [is] in thy power; only upon himself put not forth thine hand. So Satan went forth from the presence of the LORD.
Job 1:10-12

One of my favorite stories in the Bible is of a powerful man named Job. I love his story because I believe I can relate to some of the pain that he had to have been in as a result of being covered in painful boils from the crown of his head to the soles of his feet. He was tested and tried *because* he was an upright and blameless man in the sight of God. Job lost everything that he had; his livestock, his money, his children, and his health. His faith was tested and although God allowed the devil to touch Job's things, God never gave Satan permission to take his life. If you study Job carefully, however, you will learn that no part of his trials were about his "stuff"; it was all about his integrity and character. The devil wanted Job to curse God. The devil wanted to taint and distort Job's character as an upright and blameless man of God. The devil can touch your "stuff" but he cannot destroy your life. Christ has already paid with His life so you may live and breathe, so nothing and no one can lay any claim to you. You are free!

He replied, "You are talking like a foolish woman. Shall we accept good from God, and not trouble?" In all this, Job did not sin in what he said.
Job 2:10

This story demonstrates how to be weary and still stand; become angry and still stand; fall on hard times and still stand! You still praise, you still worship and you don't give up despite the situation and circumstances. Job was rooted in his faith. He had the tenacity of faith and character to remain obedient in the face of pain and suffering. Job made Satan out to be a liar and maintained his pure heart toward God. As a reward for his faithfulness, Job received twice as much livestock, servants, money and children, and he lived to be 140 years old. Job got

double for his trouble because he made a decision to persevere.
And the Lord restored Job's losses when he prayed for his friends.
Indeed the Lord gave Job twice as much as he had before
Job 42:10:

It is time for you to hold on to God's unchanging hand. Let His nail–scarred hands be a reminder that He paid the ultimate price so you can live a life of health, wealth, peace, and abundance. Trials and tribulation will come, but Christ will give you the strength to withstand. Some things in life are designed to make you stronger, wiser and build your faith in God.

And let us not be weary in well doing: for in due season we shall reap, if we faint not.
Galatians 6:9

There are too many believers growing weak and losing hope before their due season. Your due season is your expected and planned season. There will be trials and tribulations. However, there will also be the seasons when you receive what rightfully belongs to you. Remember long suffering is a fruit of the spirit. The Bible never mentioned "forever suffering" so it is sure that troubles do have an expiration date.

Fight the good fight of Faith.
1Timothy 6:12

The power of this scripture is that it shows us that there are good fights and there are bad fights. This realization actually changed my way of thinking about battles. If you have been in Church more than one time, then you have likely heard the phrase, "Fight the good fight of Faith", but do you really understand what it means? Let's examine the words "good", "fight" and "faith"

> ***Good-*** <u>Morally excellent; high quality</u>; well
> behaved, kind, honorable, educated, refined
> and sounded

Fight- A battle or combat, struggle, ability, will, to subdue, defeat or destroy, to strive vigorously and to carry on

Faith- Confidence, loyalty, trust, strong belief and truth.

Therefore, a good fight of faith is a morally excellent battle that is fought with confidence in the truth that God will do all He said He would do. You can be assured that if you strive vigorously, you will subdue and overtake your enemy because your Weapon is of the highest quality, and you serve the Supreme General of Loyalty, in whom you assuredly trust. By nature, fights, battles and combat are difficult and hard-fought. However, God has given you the ability and the will to fight. God gives you supernatural power to withstand the attacks of the enemy. Your victory is assured if you would but persevere until the end.

> *Faith is the substance of things hoped for,*
> *the evidence of things not seen.*
> ***Hebrew 11:1***

Fighting the good fight of faith also means not speaking words of death over yourself or your situation, but speaking life to your destiny and making it manifest. Endure as a solider of the Lord and God is going to honor your strength and tenacity. God has equipped you with all the tools you need to win. After each fight, you will grow in understanding, as all battles are designed to strengthen your faith in God.

Stay in pursuit of your dreams. Never give up on God or yourself. Never stop believing or trusting. Hey, just because it did not work the first time doesn't mean it won't work the next time. Press toward your goals. Focus on your vision. Stop looking to your past. Reach forward and allow God to expand, enlarge and increase you because of your obedience to Him.

"Brethren, I do not count myself to have apprehended; but one thing

*I do, forgetting those things which are behind and reaching forward
to those things which are ahead, I press toward the goal for the prize
of the upward call of God in Christ Jesus."*
Philippians 3:13-14

You will never reach your promised land if you keep looking and
reaching back. If God wanted us to keep looking back, He would have
created us with eyes in the back of our heads. Everything you need is
right in front of you. It's time to press and pull forward. God sees
where you are right now and He will meet you where you are.
Encourage yourself in the valley because God is there also. God is
creating in you a clean heart and renewing a right spirit within you.
You have been appointed, anointed and created for such a time as this.
Just stay in position with Christ. Wait on the Lord.

*And the LORD said unto (Moses), What [is] that in thine hand?
And he said, "a rod".*
Exodus 4:2

Waiting on the Lord means that you expect that all of His promises will
come to pass, despite what it looks like. Wait expectantly for His
promises to come to pass. This is not a passive, moping type of
waiting. This is you actively engaging your faith and working the plan
that He has given you, with the resources that he provides. Moses had
a staff; Sampson, the jawbone of an ass. Whatever God has promised
you, will surely come to pass. God said in His word that He will bless
whatever your hands find to do. Plead the Blood of Jesus over your
efforts, declare the Word of God and activate your faith. Don't worry
or stress about the end result because it is already done. Just wait for
your harvest, for your yield is on the way.

Perseverance is not easy, but it is the only way to actually attain the
promises of God. Below is a prayer that will help you to stand through
your storms:

*Heavenly Father, I enter into Your presence through the blood of Jesus.
I love You today and I repent for my sins. The known and unknown
things I have said, thought and done that did not line up with Your will.*

I celebrate Your goodness and Your loving kindness today. You are faithful and just. Thank You for reigning, ruling and abiding in my life. You are my keeper and my joy. I thank You for giving me strength to continue on in my assignment. When I am weak, make me strong. When I am sick, heal me by the blood of the Lamb. I know You were wounded for my transgressions and bruised for my iniquities. Thank You for building in me character, integrity and tenacity. I thank You for duplicating Yourself in me to be a beacon of light to shine in a dark place. Thank You for being my Victory and my Way Maker. I trust You to see me through in Jesus' name! I love You, Lord. I adore You Lord. I surrender my will and my life to You. Change me, Oh God! Thank You for breathing into me the gift of Your Son Jesus. Amen.

My God! You need to give God praise right now for the next level in your life! Change will always happen. You must learn to stand firm in your beliefs and convictions. Endure to the end.

You are an individual of Perseverance!

Chapter 7

Prosperity
"The Provision"

(Make this declaration out loud and with vigor!)

Devil Take Your Hands Off Of Me!!!! Take it off my finances, my increase, my expansion, my territory, my mind, my spirit and my ability to execute. I am debt free, I have increase and I am expanding in every area of my life. I am wealthy, not just financially but physically, mentally, emotionally and spiritually. I receive everything that rightfully belongs to me right now! I have a Kingdom right to be rich. I have a Kingdom right to be wealthy. I have a Kingdom right to be healthy. I have a Kingdom right to have the mind of Christ. I have a Kingdom right to walk in total deliverance. I receive my inheritance now! I am a good steward of all of my finances! I am a living testimony that my financial situation has changed for my favor! I have the ability, the power, the energy and the driving force to get and keep wealth!

But without faith [it is] impossible to please [him]: for he that cometh to God must believe that he is, and [that] he is a rewarder of them that diligently seek him.
Hebrews 11:6

I won't be broke another day in my life! I will no longer rob Peter to

pay Paul! I will exercise self-control and temperance, and no longer over-spend and live outside of my means! I no longer covet what others have nor compare myself to them! I will not make negative declarations over my life. I will no longer think small. I will no longer think poor. I am calling those things that are not as though they are. I am praising God in advance for what He is doing and for what He will continue to do in my life and in the lives of people around me! These things I declare in Jesus' name! I believe it, I declare it and it is so! Amen!!

Your words are powerful and have substance. This declaration has been released into the atmosphere so wealth must change hands. The wicked need not continue to store up your wealth for you. You are perfectly capable of managing it yourself! I am in expectation of the great things to come. Are you?

> *Beloved, I wish above all things that thou mayest prosper and be in health, even as thy soul prospereth.*
> ### *3 John 1:2*

Prosperity is a condition of being. It is a state of mind and is evidenced by successful, flourishing, or thriving states, despite any specific situation, but particularly as it relates to finances, respect and good fortune. Based on this definition, you are prosperous just because you believe you are! If you declare that you are wealthy, healthy and growing then you are wealthy, healthy and growing! You are in a blessed and prosperous state of mind and position. Now that's a powerful statement!

> *The blessings of the Lord, it maketh rich,*
> *and he addeth no sorrow with it.*
> ### *Proverbs 10:22*

The blessing of the Lord causes one to be abundantly supplied and adds no grief or pain to it. This lets me know that money can also be associated with pain. In addition, it also tells me that there is another kind of empowerment out there that is not from God. This scripture is clearly stating, the *blessings of the Lord*. It's making a distinction.

There are people who have riches who commit suicide every day. There are also people who have money but are in poor health, or suffering from sicknesses and diseases which are incurable. All of the money in the world won't pay for healing. There are people who have million dollar ideas and inventions, but crippling fear stops them from taking the steps needed to birth them out, which would allow them to live a maximized life. So, yes there can be a pain associated with riches. Money can't buy everything and it won't solve all your problems. Money is a tool, a resource, a gift and a reward. You receive money to help others, to build kingdoms and to be a problem solver. You must never forget that God is the source. Money cannot and will not buy you peace, favor, grace or faith.

But seek first the kingdom of God and His righteousness, and all these things shall be added to you.
Matthew 6:33

I have seen people run after money so much so that it has destroyed friendships, relationships, anointing, integrity and character. It amazes me that some people will even put their relationship with Christ on the line for a dollar bill. If Christ is not first in your life, then you have already lost. Success is not about only having *things;* it's about being whole in every area of Life. If you don't have a relationship that is prosperous with Christ, how do you expect to have prosperous relationships with the world?

Too many times we seek money and riches first and the Bible clearly states that we ought to seek the Kingdom of God first. You may ask, "What is the kingdom?" The kingdom is God's way of doing things. The things that will be added are His Provisions, His Promises and His Presence.

Let me tell you how God took me from Egypt to the Promise Land. Be patient and stay with me. This will bless you and increase your faith for finances! God has shown me that every level of faith He brings you to, it is strategically designed for you to trust Him like never before.

In 2006, I began to pray that God do something supernatural in my life.

I desired changed like never before. I did not want to pray the same, live the same, talk the same or remain the same. I wanted to be changed in a way that provoked me to do something different. One day, my best friend, Ruth Graham, told me that she was relocating to Georgia. This was a surprise to me because in all the time that our friendship was growing Ruth never mentioned leaving Miami. I was happy for her because I've always known her to be wise and resourceful and I knew that if she was going to make a move like that it would only be because God told her that it was what He wanted her to do. I was also a little bit sad, though, because we had laid such a good foundation for our young friendship and now she was leaving. I felt like I was literally losing my best friend. We did everything together! We talked every night on the phone sharing our hearts and desires with one another; we went shopping and just generally enjoyed hanging out with each other. Now she was leaving. What was I going to do?

Ruth was very excited about her new life and I was happy for her. I figured I could spend the time we had left hanging out together, moping about her leaving, or I could celebrate her victory with her. We started shopping for furniture and accessories for her new house while she was still in Miami. One day we were browsing some online furniture stores when I pointed out a set that I liked for myself. I told Ruth that if I had my own place, that's the set that I would put in my bedroom. She thought it was nice, too and we just kept right on browsing and talking. I knew that her moving date was fast approaching, so I was determined to make the most of our last few weeks together. Finally it was time for Ruth to move. We gave her a beautiful going away party and sent her off with all of our love, peace and happiness.

Ruth was doing very well in her new home just outside of Atlanta and we were still talking on the phone every day, but it wasn't the same as when she was home and we could hang out. A few weeks after she moved, during one of our marathon phone sessions, Ruth asked me if I would come up and help her decorate her new place. Well you know that was right up my alley! I was excited and she booked my ticket right away. I got to Atlanta in August of 2006 for my weeklong visit.

It was just like old times! We shopped, shopped and shopped some more. We spent day and night buying new stuff for the house. Our tastes are similar so everything was coming together very nicely. Later that week the furniture began to arrive, and room by room and piece by piece the house was really coming together! We were seeing the fruit of our labor and the faithfulness of God. You see there is a process associated with your blessing. You have to do something to get something. Hallelujah! One day the furniture delivery men showed up to set up one of the bedrooms. Once it started being put together I realized that it was the bedroom set that I said that I liked when we were browsing the online store! A wave of emotion rushed over me. Ruth looked at me and said, "Yes, God told me to tell you to come and live with me." I couldn't believe it. I didn't know what to do or say. My mind instantly became flood with thoughts and questions. What about my job? My doctors? The treatments for my skin? My family? My little sister? My church and my ministry?

"I don't know about this." I said. She said, "Why not?! You have been praying for change, haven't you?" "Look", she continued, "I can bring you to the table but I can't make you eat." That was a defining moment in my life. Something turned in my stomach from that statement and I knew that this was it. I began to speak to encourage myself. I had been praying and believing God for change. It felt like this was my divine connection and golden opportunity. Even knowing all of that, I still wanted to think about it.

Trust in the LORD with all your heart, and lean not on your own understanding; In all your ways acknowledge Him, And He shall direct your paths.
Proverbs 3:5-6

When I went back home to Miami, the question was still on the table without an answer. God, do I trust You enough to make this move of faith? Do I trust You enough to leave my mother's house and be on my own in a strange city? Lord, I have trusted you to direct my paths. My understanding is fearful but when I trust You, I become fearless. I continued to pray and the more I prayed the clearer the voice of the Holy Spirit became.

Now the Lord is the Spirit, and where the Spirit of the Lord is,
there is freedom.
2 Corinthians 3:17

In other words, there is liberty for you to choose. I heard the Holy Spirit say, "You have options, Lakeisha. I have presented them before you." When God is in a decision, the peace of God begins to overtake any doubt you may have had about what He has called you to do. This was it. I had a made up mind. I was moving to Georgia! Still somewhat fearful, I called Ruth and said, "Ok, let's pray and fast for 6 months. If this is of God, I will be packing my car and leaving in March." We prayed and fasted every Wednesday from September to February. We really wanted to be sure that we were in God's will. We had heard horror stories about friends who became roommates ending up enemies and I didn't want that to happen to us. I started slowly telling my family and friends what I had decided to do. Some people were happy for me and some waxed cold with negativity. The negative people told me everything bad that could happen. That's when I realized, If God said, "Yes", then I was moving despite the opinions of others. This was not about me; this is about my purpose and destiny. Execution time was near and I was ready to be used by God.

Commit to the LORD whatever you do,
and he will establish your plans.
Proverbs 16:3

Most of my close friends and relatives were excited for me. My little sister was not as thrilled that I was leaving, but she was happy for me. My father was not at all amused. I am his only child and he was not excited about me moving so far away from him. I knew and expected that this move away from my family and friends would be slightly uncomfortable, but I trusted Ruth and I believed God. I told my doctor and my pastor and gave my job one month's notice before I was ready to go. The next thing for me to do was to pass the Florida real estate exam, which I had already failed **six times**! Yes, six times.

One day another one of my best friends Sasha Miller wanted to hang out with me before I left so we decided to go out to dinner. She blessed me when she said, "Lakeisha, I prayed and ask God how can I help you?" She touched me when she handed me a gift card for $300! She told me that God said she was to deposit money into my account every two weeks. I was speechless! I was completely floored. She consulted God to find out how He wanted her to *bless me!* Now this is a place where you can really give God some praise... I know I did! Even though this is my story, don't miss the revelation in this though, I am on to something here. If He did it for me, He will surely do it for you! Glory be to God! Hallelujah!

For ye shall go out with joy, and be led forth with peace: the mountains and the hills shall break forth before you into singing, and all the trees of the field shall clap [their] hands.
Isaiah 55:12

A few days later, my close friends and family planned a surprise going away party for me. God was really showing off in this situation! He was confirming this move for me all over the place. I couldn't have been happier. When I reached the venue, my family had even laid out a red carpet for me! I heard *Mary Mary's song "Shackles"* as I was walking in. I literally wanted to breakdown but I managed to keep it together. That night I collected over $800 in cash. This was turning out to be one of the best decisions that I could have made for myself!

Now to Him who is able to do exceedingly abundantly above all that we ask or think, according to the power that works in us
Ephesians 3:20

It was finally time for me to go and take my real estate exam – *again!* I was a little apprehensive, but I felt like it was imperative that I passed this time because I was relying on this as my back up plan for my move to Georgia. I was very nervous. I reminded Jesus that I needed this since I was leaving the next day to move to Georgia! This was my seventh attempt to pass this test. Now, the number seven represents the number of completion and perfection, so needless to say, I passed that test and I was jumping for joy! I rented a car that night and packed up everything I could fit into mine and my rental cars and we were on the way. I felt like I was starting a brand new life March 17, 2007. I knew that this move was for me and I was not going to let fear stop me from writing the next chapter of my life. I had taken the first step away from

common and toward uncommon. I was in search of something that was missing in me; a piece that would launch me into destiny.

> *Now the LORD had said to Abram: "Get out of your country, from your family and from your father's house, to a land that I will show you. I will make you a great nation; I will bless you and make your name great; and you shall be a blessing. I will bless those who bless you, and I will curse him who curses you; and in you all the families of the earth shall be blessed."*
> ### *Genesis 12:1-3*

I could not have been more excited and terrified! I had made my decision and now I was making my move. I had consulted with Lord, I had received my answer, I had planned carefully, my family and close friends were in support of me and now I was on my way. I was ready to receive all that God had for me, because I had stepped out on faith. When I got to Georgia, God provided all of my medication free of charge. I had about 6 months of savings in my account. I knew that it would not take me long to find a job. I was licensed to sell real estate license in Florida and Georgia. I was going to be just fine... or so I thought. Every season of life, will be a defining moment, a stretching moment and a testing of your faith moment. After about 6 months, my finances had dried up; I still had not found a job and had no prospects for real estate. My life had changed for sure, but I couldn't see any good in this season of drought that I was in. Instinctively I knew that I was getting ready to enter into a season that would require great faith.

I ended up having to apply for and receiving government assistance. This seemed like the lowest point of my life. I had been working since I was 15 years old, paid my own taxes, and now here I was at 28 years old, sitting in the welfare office applying for Food Stamps. This was a truly humbling experience, as was my having to ask my roommate for $2 just to buy soap. I was feeling really low. In order to receive my monthly food stamp allotment of $168 and a $30 stipend for gas, I had to volunteer at the welfare office 3 days a week. Now, let me say thank God that we live in a country where there IS a food stamp office and I do not mean to insult anyone who needs to make use of the service. I am sharing my story and giving you a glimpse of how I felt at the time.

I was not happy to be on welfare but I had to swallow my pride because I needed the help. I have to say, though, that the treatment that I received was demoralizing and demeaning, which is exactly how the devil wanted me to feel.

To keep some of my dignity, I started a house cleaning business. I knew that it wouldn't pay much but I wanted to carry my own weight. Even in that, though, I had some major challenges. I was once hired to clean a house over 4,500 square feet. I cannot say if the family was actually living in the house, but I can tell you that it was filthy! I'm talking about the type of filth that should attract the attention of the health department. There were maggots in the kitchen, the bathrooms were filthy, the floors were covered in a nasty film and there was a heavily soiled laundry room. I negotiated a flat fee of $450 to be paid upon my completion of the home. That may seem like a lot, but the condition and size of the house made that price a bargain for him. I labored for over 13 hours cleaning filth like I had never seen before. When I was done, the house looked almost new. I should have been ready for what happened next. He started to complain that the house wasn't as clean as he'd hoped it would be! After some back and forth between the two of us, he told me that he only had $125 of my money! I couldn't believe it. This man had just stolen my time, my dignity and my money! Everything in me wanted to "lay hands" on him – and I don't mean in a spiritual sense… I wanted to beat the devil out of him! My heart was broken, my pride was injured and I just wanted to scream! God was still humbling me. I was being pushed, pulled and stretched in ways that I didn't know that I could be pushed, pulled and stretched.

As if all of this weren't bad enough, I even had a real estate transaction to go bad. I had been working with these buyers for months looking for houses, looking at houses, identifying financing options and everything else associated with buying a home. We finally found the perfect house for them. We made an offer, it was accepted and we set a date to close. Finally! I was beginning to feel like this was it. I would use the proceeds from my commission to be able to get myself back on my feet and finally start paying my own way. But, of course, it still wasn't my time yet. On the day of the closing, despite all of my time

energy and preparation with these buyers, they showed up with no money to cover their closing costs! I had been so specific when we wrote the contract and in all of our interactions, and yet they still showed up with no money. I ended up not earning any commissions off of that closing. I still felt like I could work it out with them because they were referred to me by a mutual friend, but that didn't work out either. Yes, foolish and complete ignorance on my part, but I believed that God would make all of this work together for my good. I have to admit, though, that by this time I was more than a little discouraged. I continued, though, to stand on the uncompromising Word of God. I just knew that this would have to get better.

I call on the LORD in my distress, and he answers me.
Psalm 120:1

After all of the disappointments and best laid plans coming to naught, I was still willing to stand. I decided that I would simply trust God. One thing that's sure about Jesus is that He is near to those who call upon His name. The Word works if you work it, so I decided to work it! First, I became wealthy and rich in my mind. I started to see myself with substance and material gain. Then the Word began to penetrate my heart. From my heart, I began to speak victory. I started confessing the Word of God and I am telling you, miracles began to take place. And then it began to happen! God started to provide for me in more ways than I can count!

A good man brings good things out of the good stored up in his heart, and an evil man brings evil things out of the evil stored up in his heart. For the mouth speaks what the heart is full of.
Luke 6:45

In other words, whatever your heart is full of is what you will speak. If your heart is filled with despair, evil, anger, poverty, hurt and frustration then that is what you will speak. However, if your heart is filled with faith, joy, peace, love, and the Word then that is what will be your manifestation once you speak it.

Spiritually, I was growing but I was challenged financially. My financial hardship showed me a whole new way of living, trusting and believing God. I began to seek the face of God like never before. My prayers changed and I began to see instant results in my life and the lives of others through prayer. I prayed and stayed in God's face and presence. God used me in ministry, outside the four walls of the church and on social media. I was teaching the Gospel of Jesus Christ. I have learned not to curse small beginnings. I learned to celebrate small victories because I knew the large victories were only a prayer away. God built me up in my most Holy Faith. My faith became steadfast and unmovable. I was flourishing spiritually. I was rich in my spirit, emotionally, physically and mentally. I was just waiting on the finances to come. I knew it was only a matter of time.

God began to provide finances for me through people. Yes, God uses people. Sasha deposited money into my account every two weeks. I didn't have to call or ask her for money nor did she call and ask did I need money; she knew I wasn't working and things were tough. Every two weeks, I knew that if no one else sent me anything, my best friend Sasha was going to come through, which she continued to do for about 17 months. I began to attend different networking events for real estate and started winning prizes. I won $250 to restaurants, $500 visa gift cards and other perks. To receive these blessings, though, I had to lose my pride. I was used to working and providing for myself. I knew that if I wanted God to do anything for me, though, that I was going to have to humble myself before Him.

I remember having to call friends and family and asking for help because I was at a place of despair. I knew that God used people to bless other people, and I knew that I had to open my mouth and ask for help in spite of the shame, the embarrassment and pride. I had to accept that it was ok to say that I needed help. I had to allow God to complete His perfect will in my life and realize that I was not in an eternal situation. What I was seeing was only temporary, according to my faith. My family and friends had been supportive of me already, but they really started to give me material help. I mean the support and love I receive from my family and friends was overwhelming. I don't even want to get into naming folks because I wouldn't want to leave anyone out. I won't forget, though, how God used some people who I

least expected Him to use, and did not use some people who I expected He would. That is just like Him, though. All glory belongs to Him. Hallelujah!

It wasn't long before things really began to turn around. I am a firm believer of sowing and reaping. I give because I love the Lord. Even in the midst of my financial drought, I retuned my tithes from the money that was given to me. There was one time when I was in church with only $11 in my bank account. I decided that I was going to sow every dime of that $11. It was the last money that I had, but giving is a heart issue for me. Don't you know that God honored my sacrifice and within 7 days God gave me a harvest of $1,100! Hallelujah! I have told you before, I see miracles in my life all of the time! I give cheerfully and grace abounds towards me. Glory!

But this I say: He who sows sparingly will also reap sparingly, and he who sows bountifully will also reap bountifully. So let each one give as he purposes in his heart, not grudgingly or of necessity; for God loves a cheerful giver. And God is able to make all grace abound toward you, that you, always having all sufficiency in all things, may have abundance for every good work.
2 Corinthians 9:6-8

I could not take the system's way of doing things any longer, so one day while toiling away at the food stamp office I told God, "If you don't provide for me I won't eat." I walked away from food stamps that same week. Two weeks later, after not working for a year and six months, I was offered a position with a large insurance company. How do I know it was God and not just a coincidence? Well, the company was looking for candidates who had college degrees and previous insurance experience. I did not have either of those things, but I had the favor of God on my life! Hallelujah! God's will outweighs any man made requirements or qualifications. He showed up and showed out on my behalf!

And my God shall supply all your need according to His riches in glory by Christ Jesus.
Philippians 4:19

In that same year, God brought back a real estate client that I had met over a year ago. She advised me that God told her that I was her realtor. This time I knew exactly what to do and how not to let what happened to me before to ever happen again. I found them the perfect home and my commission on that house was over $14,000. I sowed half of my commission into my best friend Ruth's life. Just for allowing me to say with her and not paying a dime. I was only buying food. I was so happy to attend Church to pay my tithes. I wanted to run around and shout because I knew what I had come through. The faithfulness of my patience and faith was rewarded. I was overwhelmed.

Therefore do not cast away your confidence, which has great reward.
For you have need of endurance, so that after you have done the will
of God, you may receive the promise.
Hebrew 10:35-36

This is why in spite of what I saw I could not give up on God and my ability to do better and live greater. I had to get to a place in God where I made a decision that I was going to keep speaking the Word in spite of what I was seeing at the moment. I had to open my mouth and declare something great. I had to believe that God would enlarge my territory. He expanded me beyond measure. He has increased me and enriched my life. I learned to never allow what I see to kill the vision and dreams that God has promised me. It will come to pass.

Jabez cried out to the God of Israel, "Oh that you would bless me
and enlarge my territory! Let your hand be with me, and keep me
from harm so that I will be free from pain."
And God granted his request.
1Chronicles 4:9

I have gotten to a place in my life where I speak what I want according to the Word of God and I plead the blood of Jesus over it. The devil is trying to stop me from thinking, speaking and living in the abundance that God has for me. The time is now for me to win because Christ has already won! You can do it, too! Everything in life will require you to trust, hope and believe. In other words, you must have faith. Stop cursing your destiny, begin right now. Pray that God will give you a

successful plan of action and then get up, stand up and work the plan and watch those seeds began to grow. Your destiny will become manifest. You are truly a winner. You have got to own it, believe it, work it and receive the fruits of your labor. A blessing is not always someone giving into your hands. A blessing is being empowered in every area of your life. I don't know about you but I pray that God will make me the lender and not the borrower. I want to be the one who is able to provide seed to someone else so they can began to kill some weeds in their garden of life.

My story of overcoming victory isn't over yet. I have one more tale to tell! In December 2008, I was introduced to a multi-level marketing company for the first time. Without really understanding how MLM's worked at the time, I was so impressed with the product that I invested the required $300. I believed in the product and I knew that if this product could change my life that it would definitely be able to help hundreds if not thousands of people to transform their lives. By the end of January of 2009, I had retailed over $3,000, which means that I sold over $3,000 worth of product at a profit for myself. I worked hard because I knew that this was my season to maximize on success and financial gain. I worked my 9-5 and on weekends worked my side hustle. Once I got a complete understanding of the business model, then I began to recruit others and quickly built a team, which allowed me and all of the people on my team to quickly move through the ranks of this organization and start earning very large bonuses and commissions in our spare time. Money began to flow into my life like it never had before. I was building a team as quickly as I could count them. I am not telling you this to brag but to encourage you to keep on moving and shaking because can't nobody stop you from receiving the promises but you.

And you shall remember the LORD your God, for it is He who gives you power to get wealth that He may establish His covenant which He swore to your fathers, as it is this day.
Deuteronomy 8:18

By my sixth month in this business, I was earning 5-figure paychecks on a monthly basis! The products and compensation plan changed my life in positive ways, but I never forgot that it was God who gave me the power (the energy, driving force and ability) to get wealth. At one point, the engine in my car blew out and I needed a new car. I decided that I did not want any car payments, so I saved up two pay checks from my multi-level marketing company and walked onto a new car lot and picked out my brand new car and paid cash for it – no car payments! Within 1 year I went from getting food stamps, to building a team of champs. I went from sowing my last $11 to sowing hundreds and thousands. I went from having no job to resigning from a job and becoming an entrepreneur. I had corporate leaders calling me to pray on a corporate business call. God was using me like never before. God knew that He could trust me with a little, which is why He knew that He could trust me with much. God is so much bigger than what we think. Jeremiah 29:11 tells us:

For I know the thoughts that I think toward you, saith the LORD, thoughts of peace, and not of evil, to give you an expected end.
Jeremiah 29:11

God knows the end from the beginning and thank God that He doesn't reveal it to us. Can you imagine if He did? Most of us would never move to do anything. We would remain stagnated and rooted in fear. If God showed us what we had to go through and overcome just to get to our expected end, we probably would have said, "Never mind, Lord. I don't want it anymore!" I thank God that He knew the plan that he had for me from the beginning! Hallelujah!

Go ahead and give God your best praise right now for your breakthrough! This book is anointed to destroy yokes by the power of the blood of Jesus. I am not just talking; I have walked this thing out. A lot of people want what's in God's hand but they are not willing to seek His face. Don't let this be you. You have to get to a place in God to where you can praise Him in good times and in challenged times. Hallelujah! Prosperity and provision are looking for YOU right now.

I declare to you that are walking in increase right now! I declare that your mind is lining up with the Word of God right now. I declare breakthrough for you

*in your finances, healing in your body and mind,
spiritual growth, revelation, and mental and
emotional soundness in the name of Jesus! I declare
and decree that every vessel who is reading this book
be released NOW from the spirit of infirmity, disease,
afflictions, lack and poverty. Satan, you have no
power or authority over the people of God! I bind you
and cast you out from the root by the blood of Jesus!
You have no place robbing God's people of their
blessings and inheritance!*

Hallelujah! You have got to believe it and receive it in Jesus
name.

See, God will send people to speak blessings and victory into your life.
One of my faithful and best friends, Susan Cambridge, said to me one
day, "You are chasing after everything except what's in your hands."
She would always encourage me to do the things that I am good at
doing. She would always tell me that my wealth is connected to my
writings. She said that healing is in my hands spiritually through
writing, and physically through laying of hands. I believed that, but
still I refused to write until years later.

*And Samuel said, Hath the LORD [as great] delight in burnt
offerings and sacrifices, as in obeying the voice of the LORD?
Behold, to obey [is] better than sacrifice, [and]
to hearken than the fat of rams.*
1Samuel 15:22

I had to get the revelation that there are blessings attached to
obedience. Being blessed means to be whole and empowered to
prosper. Learn to submit to the obedience of Christ and allow God's
blessing to penetrate your heart and mind and reap the rewards of
obedience.

*If you fully obey the LORD your God and carefully follow all his
commands I give you today, the LORD your God will set you high
above all the nations on earth. All these blessings will come on you
and accompany you if you obey the LORD your God:*

You will be blessed in the city and blessed in the country.

*The fruit of your womb will be blessed, and the crops of your land
and the young of your livestock—the calves of your herds and the
lambs of your flocks.*

Your basket and your kneading trough will be blessed.

You will be blessed when you come in and blessed when you go out.

*The LORD will grant that the enemies who rise up against you will
be defeated before you. They will come at you from one direction but
flee from you in seven.*

*The LORD will send a blessing on your barns and on everything you
put your hand to. The LORD your God will bless you in the land he
is giving you.*

*The LORD will establish you as his holy people, as he promised you
on oath, if you keep the commands of the LORD your God and walk
in obedience to him. Then all the peoples on earth will see that you
are called by the name of the LORD, and they will fear you. The
LORD will grant you abundant prosperity—in the fruit of your womb,
the young of your livestock and the crops of your ground—in the land
he swore to your ancestors to give you.*

*The LORD will open the heavens, the storehouse of his bounty, to
send rain on your land in season and to bless all the work of your
hands. You will lend too many nations but will borrow from none.
The LORD will make you the head, not the tail. If you pay attention
to the commands of the LORD your God that I give you this day and
carefully follow them, you will always be at the top, never at the
bottom. Do not turn aside from any of the commands I give you
today, to the right or to the left,
following other gods and serving them*
Deuteronomy 28:1-12

I am excited about this because it deals with every part of my being. I have been obedient in my transparency. I have demonstrated through my words how I obtained the rewards of obedience, which are God's blessing on my life. I have been healed of illnesses, delivered from fear and have matured spiritually. I have also attained financial security and material gain, but these things are the least of the blessings. God, though, showed me that true prosperity exists on even deeper levels. God wants to bless you to be a blessing. He expects that you will birth forth all that he has put in you for His glory. He said in His word that He would bless your womb, which demonstrates that everything has to be imputed, gestated, incubated and then birthed out. This includes everything from natural born children to visions and dreams. Your name will be blessed in spite of the generational curses your family has dealt with. God wants to bless your going out and your coming in. Every place where you sow seed will produce a harvest. Glory Hallelujah! You no longer have to be afraid. God is doing exactly what He has promised He would do.

While we do not look at the things which are seen, but at the things which are not seen. For the things which are seen are temporary, but the things which are not seen are eternal.
2 Corinthians 4:18

Go ahead and walk in the abundance in which God has promised you. Make sure you are actively doing something in the natural to get to your destination. Enjoy the journey...

You are an individual of Prosperity!

For your final exercise, reflect on everything you have learned in these 7 chapters. Write one goal or revelation that you received for each chapter in the space below. Once you have identified a total of 7 goals and/or revelations, assign dates or timeframes to them. Once you have assigned your dates or timeframes then work backwards to develop a plan to complete or reveal each one. Once you have your plan completed, start working systematically on each goal or revelation. Once your plans are complete, what will you have accomplished? Remember, this is personal for YOU, so do not rely on anyone other than God to lead you and guide you through these exercises. Do not become discouraged if these exercises take longer than you expect. Remember, the race isn't given to the swiftest, but to the one who endures to the end. May the love of God envelop and protect you, my friend.

_____

_____

_____

_____

_____

_____

_____

_____

_____

_____

_____

_____

_____

_____

_____

_____

_____

_____

_____

_____

_____

_____

ACKNOWLEDGEMENTS

I thank the Lord Jesus Christ, my Saviour, for helping me write this book! This book was made possible through the love, support and prayers of many special family and friends. I prayed and ask God to give me a Word that would transform lives and create a hunger and thirst for kingdom living. God heard my humble cry and He imparted into me supernatural wisdom and knowledge.

I would like to thank my mom, Glenda Scavella, for loving me and supporting me all these years. You set a high standard for your children and boy oh boy did it teach me strength and endurance. You have been there for me in some of the toughest times in my life but we made it through faith and prayers. I love you. My father, William Smith Jr, I was always your little girl. You dated me first and prepared me for how a woman should be treated. Thanks for validating me first. I missed out on a lot of heartache and pain. I Love you. My stepfather Gregory Scavella, thank you for helping my mother raise me and always complimenting me for setting a standard for my life. My baby sister Anjelica Scavella, you are my pride and joy. I loved you from the moment I laid eyes on you in the hospital the day you were born. I love you even more after experiencing your strength giving birth to my nephew Santana. Keep God first and you will NEVER fail. I believe in you. I pray that you will carry the mantle of prayer and worship. To my nephew Santana, you renewed my hope in love again. Loving you is a breath of fresh air. You have inspired me to become a better woman of God. I love you. I know you were born to be a leader and a king.

I would like to thank my aunt Johnnie Mae Johnson, for your listening ear, giving heart and compassionate spirit. You are truly a jewel. I love you. My auntie, Kim Dixon, a woman of endurance, thanks for helping

my mom look after me, and showing me how to cook the best white rice ever. I love you. I would like to thank my aunt, uncles, cousins and extended family of The Dixon's, The Smith's, The Benton's, The Scavella's and The Johnson's. I love you all. I'd also, like to thank Mr Raphael & Mrs. Jacqueline Reme for loving and accepting me as your second daughter.

I would like to thank my best friends who encouraged me during this process: Ruth Graham, You have inspired me more than you will ever know. Our bond is strong because we model the biblical characters of Ruth and Naomi. Your heart is HUGE! Susan Cambridge, faithful friend, giving friend and praying friend. You are truly an overcomer and your life has taught me how to PERSEVERE. Your wisdom is uncommon and always fresh. Sasha Miller, a real angel in human form. I feel like God assigned you to my life. You have impacted my life with your compassionate and caring heart. Carolyn Fraser, we been riding since I was 16. I remember the party we had at my mom house and we both got fused out for breaking the CD player. We have traveled the world together and laughed at joy and pain. God truly had His hands on us. Hasina St. Fleur, girl sometimes I forget I have you in my corner. Your faith is limitless and your love for me and Susan is truly felt. Although, we don't talk as much, I know you are there. I love you ladies. My first friend Melinda, I have experienced some of the best childhood memories with you. We taught each other what true friendship is.

I would like to thank "The Power of 7" Keysha, Takeivia, Sherry, Lamonica, Ruth and Bree. We are Victorious! We shall reap the rewards. Love you ladies.

I cannot forget to thank Mrs. Sandra Williams Boyd. I will never forget you spoke into my life when I was 15 years old and told me that I would be the rock of my family. You prayed in tongues at night over us while we slept. It was my first time hearing the sound of tongues.

You impacted my life more than you will ever know. I am grateful. I would also like to thank Patti Neal my spiritual mother, thanks for pushing me, encouraging me and forcing me to be a better intercessor. You have always motivated me.

Special thanks to my financial contributors, Rashad & Ruth Graham, Robert Boone, Donald & Nikki Small, Dave & Kimmie Felder, Antwann Johnson, Nytia Peoples, Elreka Mullen, Artravia Johnson, Susan Cambridge, Glenda & Gregory Scavella, Willie & Johnnie Johnson, Stan & Junika Saget, Bubba & Linda Knowles, Chyna Bethley, Milton & Tracey Gibson, Reneka Ward, Mona Stewart, Iris Reed, Katrina Marshall, Roger & Patti Neal. Prayer is great but this was the season for MONEY! I am so very thankful and grateful to each and every one of you for allowing God to use you to sow into my ministry. Thanks for answering the Clarion call.

I would like to thank Pastor Cecil Lamb for laying the foundation on faith. Those principles of faith have taught me how to be unshakable and unmovable. I would also like to thank my Pastors, Gary and Maya Taylor. I have grown so much over these past 5 years. I am walking in my Kingdom Authority going from good to EXCEPTIONALLY OUTSTANDING! The entire Intercessory Prayer Team at Open Word Christian Ministries, Minister Crumpler, Elder Patti (spiritual mother), Elder Cheryl (spiritual mother), Terri, Bonita, Vanessa, Herma, Zandra, Margaret, Dorothy, Armada, Gloria, Debra, Lynette, Mechelle, Sonia, Cassandra, Obi, Tina and Cynthia. Thank you for your prayers and your encouragement. We are truly carriers of God's glory. I would also like to thank, Min Betty and Min Kathy for checking up on me through this entire process. My mentor, Nikki Small, thanks for never allowing excuses, your leadership skills and powerful prayer life has forced me to push beyond my mental abilities. Love you!

Special thanks and acknowledgments to Kristine at Exodus Design Studios, the book cover, website, logo and banner were simply amazing. Kristine, I highly recommend your services. Special thanks to my editors Mary Ellis and Cheryl Pope Clark, thanks for allowing God to use your professional skills and God given gifts to capture my vision. It was truly a pleasure working with the both of you. Kimberly Felder, not only my hair stylist but my dear friend who pushed me all the way to the finish line. You believed in this vision as if it was your own. Your prayers, your blessings and your drive to motivate me were truly above and beyond what I expected. Thanks for doing my hair for the book cover. To the best photographer in the land, Robert Ector, the photo shoot was amazing. Latasha Wright, my make-up was the bomb and Leah Taylor for styling my looks.

Lastly, I would like to thank everyone who believed in me, prayed for me and encouraged me during this journey. God did it!

Love you,

Lakeisha Dixon

You can contact Lakeisha Dixon at:
www.lakeishadixon.com for speaking engagements
or email her at lakeishamiami@aol.com

65304620R00076

Made in the USA
Charleston, SC
20 December 2016